Arne Jacobsen

Frederick A. Praeger, Publishers

New York · Washington

Tobias Faber   # ARNE JACOBSEN

BOOKS THAT MATTER

Published in the United States of America by
Frederick A. Praeger, Inc., Publishers
111 Fourth Avenue, New York 3, N. Y.
Second printing, 1966
Library of Congress Catalog Card Number: 64-16676

Die Architekturgeschichte Dänemarks hat für die Entwicklung der internationalen Baukunst keine epochemachenden Beiträge geliefert. Dänemark erhielt seine Impulse immer von den großen Kulturländern, insbesondere aus Frankreich, Italien, England, Deutschland und Holland. Wenn trotzdem von einer spezifisch dänischen Architektur die Rede ist und die dänische Baukunst der Gegenwart internationale Anerkennung genießt, dann sind die Gründe dafür vor allem in dem relativ hohen Niveau des Bauens und der guten konstruktiven und handwerklichen Qualität zu suchen. Darüber hinaus haben der kritische Sinn und die Zurückhaltung der Dänen gegenüber neuen Ideen sehr viel zu einer ausgeglichenen architektonischen Gestaltung beigetragen. Die dänischen Architekten und Bauherren haben die vielfältigen Anregungen und Eindrücke, die aus dem Ausland kamen oder die sie dort selbst gewonnen hatten, nach sorgfältiger Auswahl der Landschaft, dem Klima und den Lebensgewohnheiten ihres Landes angepaßt.

In der dänischen Landschaft gibt es keine großen Kontraste, sie ist undramatisch — es fehlen schroffe Gebirge, weite Wälder und brausende Flüsse. Es ist ein Land der feinen Nuancen mit sanften Übergängen, weichen Konturen und einer milden, freundlichen Stimmung. In den alten Heidelandschaften Mittel- und Westjütlands und an der Küste der rauhen Nordsee sind jedoch der Ernst und die Kraft der Natur zu spüren. Die waagrechte Linie dominiert. Der Horizont ist weit, der Himmel hoch, und die treibenden Wolken bestimmen den Charakter des ganzen Landes. Bei ausgeglichenem Klima wechseln milde Winde und kräftige Stürme das ganze Jahr über. In diesem offenen Land haben die Bauern ihre Höfe und Felder im Windschatten der Hügel angelegt. Die hohen Dächer über den flachen, ebenerdigen Häusern wurden weit heruntergeführt, um dem Wind möglichst wenig Angriffsfläche zu bieten. Oft umschlossen mehrere niedrige Flügel einen Hofraum.

Jahrhundertelang ist Holz das traditionelle, am meisten verwendete Baumaterial gewesen. Einst war das Land von Eichenwäldern bedeckt, und die Stämme wurden für die Fachwerkkonstruktion verwendet. Selbst als die Wälder fast gänzlich niedergelegt worden waren und das Bauholz importiert werden mußte, hat sich das Fachwerk bis weit in das letzte Jahrhundert hinein als allgemein übliche Konstruktionsform auf dem Lande erhalten. Nur Schlösser, Festungsbauten und vornehme Privathäuser wurden in Backstein errichtet. Diese Fachwerktradition hat den Sinn der Dänen für Ordnung, Rhythmus und Proportion entwickelt. Als Abstand zwischen den tragenden Pfosten war bald eine feste Größe gefunden worden, bedingt durch die allgemein verwendeten Holzquerschnitte. So konnte jeder Zimmermann Häuser verschiedener Größe und Art, entsprechend der geforderten Zahl der Achsmaße, ausführen, und der Bauherr war sicher, daß er ein vernünftiges und wohlproportioniertes Haus erhalten würde. Der feste Modul des Fachwerks erlaubte freie Wahl bei der Anordnung der Fenster, wenn nur die Gesetze dieser Konstruktion eingehalten wurden.

Erst im 19. Jahrhundert fand der Backstein Eingang für einfache Wohnbauten und landwirtschaftliche Gebäude. Aber das Prinzip der regelmäßigen Teilung beim Fachwerk führte unmerklich auch beim gemauerten Haus zu einem ebenfalls klaren Rhythmus durch die modulbestimmten Pfeilerfenster. Während des Empire um 1800 entstand eine besonders harmonische Synthese zwischen den vom Ausland übernommenen klassischen Idealen und der dänischen Bautradition. Die Folge war eine rege Bautätigkeit mit schönen verputzten und gestrichenen Häusern, bei denen die regelmäßige Anordnung und Proportionierung der Fensteröffnungen zusammen mit einer schlichten, präzisen Detaillierung architektonisch bestimmend waren.

V   Diese Zeit wurde für die dänische Architektur zu einer sehr glück-

Danish architectural history has not made any epoch-making contribution to the development of international architecture. Denmark has always received inspiration from the large centres of culture, especially France, Italy, England, Germany and Holland. If, nevertheless, we talk of a specifically Danish architecture, and if contemporary Danish architecture has gained an international reputation, the reasons must mainly be sought in the comparatively high standard of building construction and in the high quality of design and workmanship. In addition, the critical sense and moderation of the Danes in appraising new ideas have greatly contributed to the creation of a balanced architectural style. Danish architects and their clients have succeeded, after careful selection, in adapting the manifold inspirations and impressions which came from abroad, or which they themselves had gathered abroad, to the landscape, climate and living habits of their own country.

The Danish landscape shows no great contrasts; it is undramatic — there are no rugged peaks, no vast forests, no raging torrents. It is a country of fine shades and smooth transitions, flowing contours and a mild, friendly mood. In the timeless heath landscape of Central and Western Jutland and at the coast of the rough North Sea, however, the serenity and power of Nature can be felt. The horizontal line dominates. The horizon is wide, the sky is high, and the drifting clouds determine the character of the whole country. In the balanced climate, mild winds and strong gales are liable to alternate throughout the year. In this open country, the peasants have built their smallholdings and cultivated their fields in the lee of the hills. The high roofs covering the low single-storey houses were taken far down in order to minimise wind exposure. Often, a courtyard was surrounded by several low buildings.

For centuries, wood was the traditional and most frequently used building material. At one time, the country was covered by large oak forests, and the tree trunks were used for half-timbered buildings. Even when the forests had almost wholly disappeared and the timber had to be imported, the half-timbered house maintained its position far into the 19th century as the most usual type of rural structure. It was only the castles, the fortresses and the manor houses which were erected in brick. This tradition of half-timbered buildings has developed the Danish sense of neatness, rhythm and proportion. The distance between bearing struts was soon standardized, being governed by the timber sizes in general use. In this way, any carpenter was able to build houses of different sizes and types, in accordance with the specified spacings, and the client was sure to obtain a reasonable and well proportioned house. The fixed module of the half-timbered structure permitted a wide choice in the arrangement of the windows as long as the basic rules of this type of construction were observed.

It was only in the 19th century that brick came into use for simple houses and agricultural buildings. But, imperceptibly, the principle of regular spacing associated with the traditional half-timbered structure led even in the brick house to clear rhythm, owing to the adoption of module dimensions for the window pillars. During the Empire period around 1800, a particularly harmonious synthesis was achieved between the classic ideals imported from abroad, and Danish building tradition. This gave rise to a great building activity resulting in fine, plastered and painted houses, architecturally dominated by the regular arrangement and fine proportioning of the window openings and the unpretentious and precise detail work. For Danish architecture at large, this period proved to be highly felicitous. In Denmark, the ideas of classicism survived, in the 19th century, longer than in most other countries in spite of the victorious advance of industrialisation and the style imitations practised in the

lichen Periode. Die Ideen des Klassizismus haben hier im 19. Jahrhundert länger gewirkt als in den meisten anderen Ländern, trotz des Siegeszuges der Industrialisierung und der Stilnachahmungen in ganz Europa. Dänemark blieb dadurch vor den schlimmsten stilistischen Ausschweifungen dieser Zeit bewahrt. Die Forderung des Klassizismus nach Vereinfachung und Ordnung und der allgemein ausgeprägte Sinn für Natürlichkeit und Verbindlichkeit haben sich von der Empirezeit an in der dänischen Baukunst ausgewirkt und sie bis in die Gegenwart entscheidend geformt.

Die Architektur Dänemarks ist arm an großer und dramatischer Baukunst. Das Pathos lag den dänischen Architekten fern. Der starke persönliche Ausdruck wurde fast immer unterdrückt zugunsten eines mehr anonymen Wirkens. Das soll nicht heißen, daß die dänischen Architekten sich selbst verleugneten und ihre individuelle künstlerische Note nicht zu erkennen war. Es ist nicht schwierig, die beiden großen Architekten des 18. Jahrhunderts, Eigtved und Thura, voneinander zu unterscheiden, oder die Architekten des Klassizismus, Harsdorff und C. F. Hansen, den Baumeister des Thorwaldsen-Museums Bindesbøll oder Kay Fisker in unserer Zeit zu charakterisieren. Aber bei allen sind die künstlerische Disziplin, eine traditionelle Zurückhaltung, eine schamhafte Furcht vor Gefühlsduselei und Theatralik stärker gewesen als der Drang, sich selber zu manifestieren. So ist eine Architektur entstanden, die in ihrem Ausdruck zwischen verhaltener Wärme und kühlerem Intellekt wechselt. Nicht zuletzt war auch der Respekt vor der dänischen Landschaft bestimmend. Die Anpassung der Bauten an ihre Umgebung ist immer ein wesentlicher Ausgangspunkt des Entwurfs gewesen.

Das Werk Arne Jacobsens fügt sich ganz natürlich in diese Entwicklung ein. Seine Baukunst respektiert den Charakter der Landschaft als etwas Primäres. Bäume und Bepflanzung sind immer von ihm selbst als integrierender Teil der architektonischen Aufgabe genau geplant. Der klare Entwurf, die sachliche, schlichte Materialwahl, die durchgearbeiteten Details, die gute handwerkliche Ausführung und die wohlproportionierte, disziplinierte architektonische Gestaltung sind charakteristisch für seine besten Arbeiten. Während seiner bald vierzigjährigen Tätigkeit als Architekt hat Arne Jacobsen Anregungen von verschiedenen Seiten her erhalten, aber sie sind immer von ihm umgeformt und den dänischen Verhältnissen angepaßt worden. Seine Lösungen sind unverwechselbar und lassen keinen Zweifel darüber aufkommen, daß es sich um Arbeiten von ihm handelt.

Arne Jacobsen ist sozusagen mit dem Funktionalismus aufgewachsen. In seiner Ausbildungszeit folgte er allen Strömungen in der Architektur der zwanziger Jahre bis zum entscheidenden Durchbruch des Funktionalismus im Norden um 1930. Sowohl in Dänemark als auch in Schweden hatte der Neoklassizismus eine kurze und glanzvolle Periode, die kurz vor dem ersten Weltkrieg begann und bis Anfang der zwanziger Jahre dauerte. Damals scharte sich um den bedeutenden Architekten Carl Petersen und den Kunsthistoriker Vilhelm Wanscher eine begabte junge Architektengeneration mit Kay Fisker und Aage Rafn, die sich mit hohen ästhetischen Idealen der großen und reinen Architektur verschrieben hatte.

Das Interesse des Neoklassizismus reichte von der repräsentativen Monumentalarchitektur bis zur bürgerlichen Baukultur um 1800. Das Ergebnis vieler Bauaufnahmen im ganzen Lande war eine Reihe von Publikationen. Besonders die Bücher über Liselund, ein kleines romantisches Louis-XVI-Schloß auf der Insel Møn, und über den Maler, Bildhauer und Architekten Nicolaj Abildgaard (1749-1809) wurden für die jungen Architekten richtungweisend. Besonders bewundert wurde Abildgaards eigenes Haus Spurveskjul (»Spatzenversteck«) bei Kopenhagen. Das monumentale Hauptwerk des Neoklassizismus, das Polizeipräsidium, wurde 1924 fertiggestellt, ein

rest of Europe. Denmark was therefore spared the worst stylistic excesses of that time. The classicistic demands for simplification and neatness and the generally well developed sense for all that is natural and agreeable have continued to affect Danish architecture since the time of the Empire period and have, right up to the present, had a decisive influence on it.

Danish architecture is devoid of great and dramatic traits. Pathos has been alien to Danish architects. Strong personal expression has nearly always been suppressed in favour of more anonymous efforts. This does not mean that Danish architects have been self-effacing or that their individual artistic notes have not been recognisable. It is not difficult to distinguish the two great architects of the 18th century, Eigtved and Thura, or to characterize the architects of classicism, Harsdorff and C. E. Hansen, or the designer of the Thorvaldsen Museum, Bindesbøll, or Kay Fisker in our time. With all of them, however, artistic discipline, traditional moderation and a fear of appearing sentimental or theatrical have been greater than the urge to manifest themselves. In this way, an architecture has come into being which alternates in its expression between restrained warmth and cooler intellect. Not least, the respect for the Danish landscape has had a decisive effect. The adaptation of the buildings to their environments has always been an essential design factor.

Arne Jacobsen's work is well in keeping with this development. His architecture respects the character of the landscape as something of primary importance. Invariably, this landscape and the vegetation have been planned by himself as an integral part of the architectural task. Lucidity of design, objective and unostentatious choice of materials, precisely planned details, a high standard of workmanship and well proportioned, disciplined architectural forms are characteristic of his best works. During his nearly 40 years as an architect, Arne Jacobsen has received inspirations from several quarters; but they have always been transformed by him, and adapted to Danish conditions. Jacobsen's solutions are unmistakable and leave no doubt as to their authorship.

Arne Jacobsen has, as it were, grown up with functionalism. In his formative years, he followed all the architectural currents of the 1920's up to the decisive break-through of functionalism in Scandinavia around 1930. In Denmark as well as in Sweden, neo-classicism enjoyed a brief and glorious period which began shortly before World War I and persisted into the early 1920's. At that time, the leading architect Carl Petersen and the art historian Vilhelm Wanscher were surrounded by a generation of gifted young architects including Kay Fisker and Aage Rafn who, with their high aesthetic ideals, had devoted themselves to architecture great and pure.

The interests of neo-classicism ranged from representative monumental architecture to the bourgeois building tradition around 1800. The result of many surveys of buildings throughout the country was a series of publications. In particular, the descriptions of Liselund Castle, a small romantic Louis XVI palace in the island of Møn, and the books on the painter, sculptor and architect Nicolaj Abildgaard (1749-1809) had a strong influence on young architects. The object of special admiration was Abildgaard's own house "Spurveskjul" ("Sparrows' Hide-out") near Copenhagen. That monumental prototype of neo-classicistic architecture, the police headquarters in Copenhagen, was completed in 1924, one year after Arne Jacobsen had been admitted to the Academy. This building attracted the attention and admiration even of many young architects. However, in spite of all its qualities, it was a work of eclectic formalism, far removed from the currents of its time, and most people had to acknowledge that this path was leading into a cul-de-sac. Even so, neo-classicism may be said to have had an important bearing on

Jahr nach Arne Jacobsens Aufnahme in die Akademie. Dieser Bau erregte auch bei vielen jungen Architekten Aufsehen und Bewunderung. Jedoch war er trotz aller seiner Qualitäten ein Werk des eklektizistischen Formalismus, weit entfernt von den Strömungen dieser Zeit, und die meisten erkannten, daß dieser Weg in eine Sackgasse führte. Die Bedeutung des Neoklassizismus für die Zukunft lag eher darin, daß er die künstlerische Disziplin und das Gefühl für die Qualität der handwerklichen Verarbeitung geschärft hatte.

Die Begeisterung der jungen Architekten für die Ideale des Klassizismus ließ in Dänemark kein besonderes Interesse aufkommen für die zeitgenössischen Strömungen draußen in der Welt wie die Stijl-Gruppe in Holland und die Bauhaus-Bewegung in Deutschland. Aber im Laufe der zwanziger Jahre erhob sich doch eine starke Opposition gegen den klassizistischen Formalismus. Der Widerstand kam besonders wirkungsvoll in der Zeitschrift »Kritisk Revy« 1926-28 zum Ausdruck, in der das weltfremde Theoretisieren der dänischen Architekten gegeißelt wurde. Die Architekten sollten sich lieber ihrer sozialen und ökonomischen Verantwortung bei der Stadtplanung, beim Wohnungsbau usw. bewußt werden, forderte die »Kritisk Revy«. Zur gleichen Zeit wurden die Arbeiten des Bauhaus-Kreises veröffentlicht, wie auch dessen Theorien über den Zusammenhang des neuen künstlerischen Ausdrucks mit der technisch-wissenschaftlichen Entwicklung der Gegenwart. Die »Kritisk Revy« erlangte große Bedeutung zu ihrer Zeit, jedoch mehr als scharfer Kritiker der formalistischen Architektur denn als Wegbereiter einer neuen Baukunst.

Die Ideen und künstlerischen Möglichkeiten des Funktionalismus setzten sich im Norden zuerst in Schweden bei der Stockholmer Ausstellung 1930 durch, vor allem dank des hochbegabten Architekten der Ausstellung, Gunnar Asplund, der die neuen Baustoffe Stahl, Beton und Glas für eine festlich gestimmte, konstruktive Architektur ideenreich verwendete. Asplund hatte mehrere Jahre mit großem Talent und Können nach klassizistischen Idealen gearbeitet und war nicht Funktionalist im eigentlichen Sinne. Aber er war ein großer Künstler, der die Impulse der neuesten Architektur des Auslandes, die im Einklang mit dem Charakter der Ausstellungsaufgabe standen, aufzugreifen und auszunutzen verstand. Die funktionalistische Formsprache war in den späten zwanziger Jahren schon in begrenztem Maße in Dänemark eingedrungen, aber bei dem für jene Jahre bezeichnenden engen Kontakt zwischen dänischer und schwedischer Architektur wirkte die Stockholmer Ausstellung trotzdem auf die jungen dänischen Architekten wie eine Fanfare, die eine glückliche Zeit verkündete. Die neue Formsprache wurde begeistert von ihnen aufgegriffen, zwar in vielen Fällen kritikloser als es sonst in ihrem Lande üblich war, aber doch auch mit wachem Verständnis für die Anpassung an dänische Verhältnisse.

Mit seiner aufnahmebereiten Begabung folgte Arne Jacobsen als junger Student und als Architekt diesen Ideen, von der Schwärmerei für die Abildgaard-Zeit bis zur Begeisterung für die kubistische Architektur Le Corbusiers. Vor allem beschäftigten ihn zunächst jedoch die Möglichkeiten der äußeren Form. Die soziale und ökonomische Seite des Funktionalismus interessierte ihn weniger, und ein tieferes Verständnis für den eigentlichen Inhalt und den konstruktiven Aufbau der verschiedenen Architekturformen war ihm noch fremd. Während andere sich noch mit der Theorie auseinandersetzten, suchte Arne Jacobsen mit seinem früh entwickelten Talent und seiner Fähigkeit, sich neue Ideen schnell anzueignen, bereits die noch nicht ganz ausgereiften Gedanken zu verwirklichen. Einige hochbegabte Projekte und im Äußeren ästhetisch befriedigende Häuser machten ihn, noch nicht dreißigjährig, zu einem der vielversprechenden Architekten seiner Zeit, Seite an Seite mit den Begründern des dänischen Funktionalismus, Mogens Lassen und Vilhelm Lauritzen.

future development: — it had enhanced artistic discipline and the appreciation of good workmanship.

Because of the young architects' enthusiasm for the ideals of classicism, Denmark displayed no particular interest in contemporary currents abroad, such as the Stijl Group in Holland, and the Bauhaus Movement in Germany. During the 1920's however, there arose a strong opposition to classicistic formalism. The resistance war particularly effectively expressed during the years 1926-28 in the architectural journal "Kritisk Revy" where the Danish architects were decried as theorists sitting in an ivory tower. They were admonished to turn their attention to social and economic responsibilities in town planning, housing, etc. At the same time, publicity was given to the works of the Bauhaus Circle and to its theories on the relationship between modern artistic expression and the technological and scientific developments of the time. The journal assumed great importance in its time, more however as a sharp critic of formalistic architecture than as a torch bearer of a new architecture.

In Scandinavia, the first occasion on which the ideas and artistic potentialities of functionalism became a dominant feature was the Stockholm Exhibition, 1930; this was mainly due to the highly gifted architect of the Exhibition, Gunnar Asplund, who applied a wealth of ideas to the use of the new materials — steel, concrete and glass — thus creating a positive architecture held in a festive mood. For several years, Asplund had harnessed his great talent and knowledge to classicistic ideals, and he was not regarded as a functionalist proper. But he was a great artist who was able to absorb and utilise those impulses of the latest trends in international architecture which were in keeping with the character of the exhibition task. During the late 1920's, the formal language of functionalism had already found some limited acceptance in Denmark; even so, in view of the close contact between Danish and Swedish architecture characteristic for those years, the Stockholm Exhibition had, on the young Danish architects, the effect of a fanfare heralding a happy future. The new formal language was taken up by them with enthusiasm, though in many cases perhaps with less critical appreciation than was usual in their country; they were, however, aware of the need of adapting the style to Danish conditions

As a young student and as an architect, Arne Jacobsen with his receptive talents followed these ideas, from the admiration for the Abildgaard period to the enthusiasm for Le Corbusier's cubistic architecture. For the time being, however, he was mainly concerned with the potentialities of external design. He was less interested in the social and economic aspects of functionalism, and a deeper understanding for the substance and structure of different architectural styles was still alien to him. Whilst others were still struggling with theory, Arne Jacobsen with his early developed talent and his capacity of absorbing new ideas quickly, was already trying to give concrete form to ideas which had not yet quite matured. At an age of not yet 30 years, some projects reflecting great talent and a number of houses with aesthetically satisfactory exteriors earned him an early reputation as a contemporary architect of high promise, side by side with the founders of Danish functionalism, Mogens Lassen and Vilhelm Lauritzen.

Arne Jacobsen wurde am 11. Januar 1902 in Kopenhagen als Sohn des Großhändlers Johan Jacobsen geboren. Er zeigte früh Talent zum Zeichnen und Malen, und es war lange Zeit der Wunsch des Jungen, Maler zu werden. Sein Vater wollte ihn jedoch lieber Architekt werden lassen, und da er schon als Fünfzehnjähriger seine Schulzeit abgeschlossen hatte, mußte er den praktischen Weg — Handwerkslehre und technische Schule — wählen, um an der Kunstakademie aufgenommen zu werden. An der Technischen Schule von Kopenhagen kam er in eine Gruppe ungewöhnlich begabter junger Leute, die alle Architekten werden wollten, mit den Brüdern Mogens und Flemming Lassen an der Spitze.

In der Architekturschule der Kunstakademie wurde man schnell auf Jacobsens Zeichentalent aufmerksam, und seine Aussichten als Maler standen noch einmal zur Debatte. Aber bald fesselte ihn das Architekturstudium ganz. Kay Fisker und Ivar Bentsen wurden seine Lehrer; bei Kay Gottlob studierte er Baugeschichte. Besonders Gottlob wurde für Jacobsen wichtig, teils durch die sorgfältigen Zeichen- und Proportionsstudien der klassischen Kunst, die in der Akademie stattfanden, teils durch Studienreisen unter Gottlobs Führung nach Frankreich und Italien, an denen Jacobsen teilnahm. Auf diesen Exkursionen fertigte Jacobsen eine Reihe sehr schöner Bauaufnahmen und Aquarellskizzen an. 1927 beendete er sein Studium an der Akademie. Ein Jahr später erhielt er die kleine Goldmedaille für den Entwurf eines Nationalmuseums in Klampenborg, einem außerordentlich ansprechenden Projekt mit schlichten Baukörpern in knappen und strengen Formen. Die Inspiration durch die Arbeiten Gunnar Asplunds ist hier schon spürbar.

Während seiner Studienzeit hatte Jacobsen in verschiedenen Architekturbüros gearbeitet, so unter anderem bei Thorkel Hjejle und Niels Rosenkjær, die durch einige von der Architektur der Abildgaard-Zeit beeinflußte Einfamilienhäuser bekannt geworden waren. Jacobsen hatte großen Gewinn von der Zusammenarbeit mit dem sensiblen und begabten Rosenkjær, der noch während Jacobsens Tätigkeit in seinem Büro ganz jung starb. Später war Jacobsen drei Jahre lang im Rathaus von Kopenhagen bei Stadtarchitekt Poul Holsøe angestellt, wo er unter anderem die Bauführung von einem Musikpavillon, einigen niedrigen Schutzdächern und von Bauten mit abgewalmten Dächern auf dem Enghave-Platz in Kopenhagen innehatte.

Aber schon vor seinem Abgang von der Akademie hatte Jacobsen

Arne Jacobsen was born in Copenhagen, on 11th January 1902, as a son of the wholesale merchant Johan Jacobsen. He showed an early talent for drawing and painting and, for a long time, it was his wish to become a painter. His father, however, prompted him to become an architect, and since he had already left school at the age of 15, he had to choose the practical career, through apprenticeship and technical college, in order to be accepted by the Academy of Arts. At Copenhagen Technical College, he happened to fall in with a group of unusually gifted young men, led by the brothers Mogens and Flemming Lassen, all of whom wanted to become architects.

At the Architectural College of the Academy of Arts, Jacobsen's talent for drawing was soon discovered, and his prospects as a painter were once more under discussion. Soon, however, he was wholly attracted to the study of architecture. Kay Fisker and Ivar Bentsen became his teachers, and his studies of architectural history were directed by Kay Gottlob. The latter, in particular, was of great importance to Jacobsen, partly because of his painstaking surveys in the form of drawings and proportion studies of classicist art which took place at the Academy, and partly because of educational travels to France and Italy organised by Gottlob, in which Jacobsen took part. During these travels Jacobsen produced a number of very fine building surveys and aquarelles. His studies at the Academy were completed in 1927. A year later, he was awarded the Minor Gold Medal for the design of a National Museum to be erected in Klampenborg Cottage Park, an extremely attractive project with unpretentious buildings of strictly disciplined design. Here, the inspiration derived from the works of Gunnar Asplund is already apparent. During his Academy years, Jacobsen had already worked in several architectural bureaux, e.g. with Thorkel Hjejle and Niels Rosenkjær who had become well known through their designs for a number of detached houses, influenced by the architecture of the Abildgaard period. Jacobsen had reaped great benefit from his collaboration with the sensitive and gifted Rosenkjær who died still very young, while Jacobsen was still working in his office. Later, for a period of three years, Jacobsen worked at Copenhagen Town Hall under the City Architect, Poul Holsøe, where he was, inter alia, in charge of the construction of a music pavilion, some low shelters, and buildings with hipped roofs at Enghave Square, Copenhagen.

But even before leaving the Academy, Jacobsen had already carried out his first independent work. At the Paris World Exhibition in 1925,

»Haus der Zukunft«, 1929 (in Zusammenarbeit mit Flemming Lassen).
"House of the Future", 1929 (in collaboration with Flemming Lassen).

Haus Max Rothenborg, Ordrup, 1930.
Max Rothenborg's House, Ordrup, 1930.

seine ersten selbständigen Arbeiten ausgeführt. Auf der Weltausstellung in Paris 1925, wo er eine Silbermedaille erhielt, zeigte er einen Bucheinband und einen Stuhl. 1927 baute er beim Friedhof in Hellerup seine erste Villa für Professor Sigurd Wandel. Dieses Haus aus gelben Backsteinen und von einfacher kubischer Form ist übrigens im Detail und mit dem breiten überstehenden Dach noch von der Anmut der Abildgaard-Zeit inspiriert. Im Laufe der nächsten Jahre folgten dieser Villa, der die Gemeinde Gentofte ihre Prämie für schöne Bauten verlieh, eine Reihe Einfamilienhäuser in Gentofte. Das Vorbild der Abildgaard-Epoche wird wieder deutlich unter anderem in dem Haus M. Steensen von 1932 (unten) mit seinem segmentförmigen Frontgiebel, dem überhängenden Dach und den waagrechten Linien des Spaliers an der Fassade. Auch der Einfluß von englischen Häusern ist in diesen ersten Bauten zu spüren. Arne Jacobsen hatte Erfolg und konnte bald ein ganzes Wohnviertel in Ordrup Mose gestalten, vor allem durch eigene Bauten (Seite X), aber auch durch die Wirkung, die seine Arbeiten auf andere Architekten ausübten. Diese in wenigen Jahren fertiggestellte Bebauung bestand aus ein- und zweigeschossigen gelben Backsteinhäusern mit Ziegel- oder Eternitdächern, weißen Fensterläden oder kleineren Erkern. Er selbst baute in diesen Jahren sechs Häuser allein im Hegelsvej. Bemerkenswert ist die immer freier werdende Grundrißgestaltung mit einer weniger straffen Disposition der Fenster und größeren Fensteröffnungen für die einzelnen Räume. Aber die einzelnen Baukörper bewahrten dennoch eine gewisse Geschlossenheit und Schlichtheit.

Da sich Arne Jacobsen auch um die Bepflanzung kümmerte, konnte er großzügige Verbindungen von der Wohnung zum Garten schaffen. Er hat hier einen gemäßigt modernen Einfamilienhaustyp entwickelt, der in den dreißiger Jahren sehr populär wurde. Dieser Typ knüpfte an die dänische Bautradition an, während er gleichzeitig auch die Forderungen der Gegenwart nach einer weniger konventionellen Lebensweise, helleren und freundlicheren Räumen und Bequemlichkeit erfüllte. Arne Jacobsen hätte als Erfolgsarchitekt diese Haustypen zweifellos noch viele Jahre lang bauen können, aber auf die Dauer befriedigten ihn diese Lösungen nicht.

1925 hatte Jacobsen die Internationale Ausstellung der angewandten Künste in Paris besucht und Le Corbusiers Pavillon de l'Esprit Nouveau gesehen, der seiner Zeit weit voraus war und zu dessen Verständnis der junge Akademieschüler noch nicht die Voraussetzungen

Haus M. Steensen, Ordrup, 1932.
M. Steensen's house, Ordrup, 1932.

where he was awarded a Silver Medal, he exhibited a book cover and a chair. In 1927, he built his first villa for Professor Sigurd Wandel on a site near Hellerup Cemetery. This house of yellow brick and simple cubic shape was, in its details and with its wide overhanging roof, still inspired by the grace of the Abildgaard period; it was awarded the City of Gentofte Prize for beautiful buildings. During the next few years, this villa was followed by a number of other detached houses in Gentofte. The example of the Abildgaard period is again apparent, inter alia in the house for M. Steensen (below) with its segment-shaped front gable, and the horizontal lines of the façade trellis work. These first buildings of his also show the influence of English housing design. Arne Jacobsen was successful and was soon able to shape an entire residential district at Ordrup Mose, mainly with his own buildings (page X), but also through the influence of his work on that of other architects. This housing estate, completed within a few years, consisted of single and double storey yellow brick houses with tiled or asbestos cement roofs, white window shutters or smallish alcoves. During these years, he himself designed six houses in Hegelsvej alone. A noteworthy feature is the increasing degree of liberty in the layout design, with a less rigid window arrangement and with larger window openings for the individual rooms. Even so, the individual buildings still conveyed an impression of integrity and simplicity. Since Arne Jacobsen also took a personal interest in the flora, he was able to create dramatic transitions from dwelling to garden. He thereby developed a moderately modern type of detached house which became very popular during the 1930's. This type was in keeping with Danish building tradition whilst at the same time meeting contemporary requirements for a less conventional way of living, for brighter and friendlier rooms and greater comfort. As a successful architect, Arne Jacobsen would no doubt have been able to continue building this type of houses for many more years; in the long run, however, these solutions could not satisfy him.

In 1925, Jacobsen visited the International Exhibition for Applied Arts in Paris and saw Le Corbusier's "Pavilion de l'Esprit Nouveau" which was far in advance of its time and which the young Academy student was not yet fully able to comprehend. In 1927-28, he derived greater inspiration in Berlin from the works of Mies van der Rohe and Gropius. At the same time, Jacobsen built for himself a house in the cubic style, with smoothed, white-washed outer walls, flat roof and continuous window ribbon. This house at Gotfred Rodesvej, Ordrup, is interesting and typical for that time, but it has only a superficial likeness to the clear reinforced concrete structures of the examples by which it had been inspired. For economic reasons the house was erected in conventional Danish building materials, brick and timber, with covered steel beams above the windows. The plastered and oil-painted brickwork was intended to be taken for concrete. The house had technical flaws, and there were certain ambiguities in the use of materials — a feature also encountered in several other houses of these years, built by Jacobsen and his colleagues.

A year later, he was awarded, together with Flemming Lassen, the First Prize in a competition for a "House of the Future" (page VIII) which was built for an exhibition in Copenhagen sponsored by the Academic Association of Architects in 1929. Part of this house, circular in shape, had two storeys, with a helicopter landing ground on the roof, and the whole idea and design suggested gaiety and talent. In 1930, Jacobsen was commissioned to build a large villa for the lawyer Max Rothenborg in Ordrup (page VIII). In Mrs. Rothenborg, Jacobsen found a receptive and enthusiastic client who wholeheartedly responded to the new ideas pursued by Jacobsen and his

hatte. Stärker inspiriert wurde er 1927-28 in Berlin durch die Arbeiten von Mies van der Rohe und Gropius. Zur gleichen Zeit baute Jacobsen für sich selbst ein Haus im kubischen Stil, mit weiß gestrichenen, glatten Außenwänden, Flachdach und durchlaufendem Fensterband. Dieses Haus im Gotfred Rodesvej in Ordrup ist interessant und typisch für diese Zeit, hat aber doch nur eine oberflächliche Ähnlichkeit mit den klaren Stahlbetonkonstruktionen der Vorbilder. Aus ökonomischen Gründen war das Haus mit den traditionellen dänischen Materialien Backstein und Holz errichtet, mit verdeckten Stahlträgern über den Fenstern. Das verputzte und mit Ölfarbe gestrichene Ziegelmauerwerk sollte Beton vortäuschen. Das Haus hatte technische Mängel und auch Unklarheiten in der Materialverwendung wie verschiedene andere Häuser dieser Jahre, die von Jacobsen und seinen Kollegen gebaut worden waren.

Ein Jahr später gewann er mit Flemming Lassen einen Wettbewerb für ein »Haus der Zukunft« (Seite VIII), das auf einer von der Akademisk Arkitektforening 1929 veranstalteten Ausstellung in Kopenhagen gebaut wurde. Das kreisrunde Haus war teilweise zweigeschossig, besaß einen Helikopterlandeplatz auf dem Dach und wirkte in seiner ganzen Idee und Gestaltung lustig und talentvoll. 1930 erhielt Jacobsen den Auftrag, für den Anwalt Max Rothenborg ein großes Einfamilienhaus in Ordrup zu bauen (Seite VIII). In Frau Rothenborg fand Jacobsen eine sehr aufgeschlossene und begeisterte Bauherrin, die ganz auf die neuen Ideen Jacobsens und seiner Zeit einging, besonders bei der Einrichtung des Hauses, für die neue Möbel in genauer Übereinstimmung mit der Formensprache der Architektur entworfen wurden. Sonst waren die ersten »funktionalistischen« Häuser meist konventionell eingerichtet mit Möbeln von sehr geringer Qualität, die in schreiendem Gegensatz zur Bauform standen. Rothenborgs Haus war die bedeutendste Arbeit der frühen Jahre, leider ist es jedoch durch spätere Umbauten verdorben worden.

Öffentliche Wettbewerbe haben einen außerordentlichen Einfluß auf die Entwicklung der dänischen Architektur gehabt. In den letzten Generationen sind zahlreiche der bedeutendsten öffentlichen Bauten nach Wettbewerben vergeben worden. Die hervorragendsten Vertreter des Standes haben ebenso wie junge und unbekannte Architekten ihr ganzes Können aufgeboten, um die beste Lösung für wichtige Bauaufgaben zu finden; Ideenwettbewerbe haben neue und bessere Typen im Schulbau, Wohnungsbau und so weiter hervorgebracht.

contemporaries. This applied especially to the interior design for which new furniture strictly compatible with the formal architectural language was designed. Most of the first "functionalistic" houses had conventional sets of furniture of very low quality which was in striking contrast to the design of the building. Rothenborg's house was the most significant work of Jacobsen's early years: unfortunately it was spoilt by later conversions.

Public competitions have had an extremely important influence on the development of Danish architecture. During recent decades, the design work for many of the most important public buildings has been awarded to architects as a result of a competition. The most prominent representatives of their profession as well as young and unknown architects have made strenuous efforts to find the best solutions for important building tasks. Design competitions have yielded new and better types of schools, housing, etc. Arne Jacobsen is the outstanding example of a man who, not only as a young architect working with colleagues but also later on his own, gained his commissions by means of supreme projects submitted in response to competitions.

One of his first competition successes was a design for Bellevue Lido, Klampenborg, a project distinguished by a logical and simple layout plan. There followed, in 1933, the Bellavista housing estate opposite the Lido (page 28). The three-wing complex is adapted to the ground with supreme skill. The staggering of the façades ensures sunlight and good view for each individual dwelling. Externally, the design follows the principles of international functionalism and is, at least partly, affected by those minor structural and technical inconsistencies which are typical of the years shortly after 1930. Even so, the entire group has an air of gracefulness, and the dwellings are still in great demand.

In 1934-35, the Bellevue estate was expanded by the Bellevue Theatre, combined with a restaurant; by this time, Jacobsen had succeeded in re-shaping a major part of Old Klampenborg. Since the theatre was mainly intended for light comedy and musicals during the summer season, Jacobsen tried to endow it with the charm and lightness of the "great top" of the Circus. A particularly charming effect was obtained when the sliding roof of the auditorium was opened and the starlit sky of the summer night became visible. Unfortunately, for reasons which had nothing to do with the architect, it was found after a few years that neither the theatre nor the

Haus Gertie Wandel, Ordrup, 1934.
Gertie Wandel's House, Ordrup, 1934.

Haus Erik Dugdale, Ordrup, 1934.
Erik Dugdale's House, Ordrup, 1934.

Arne Jacobsen steht als Beispiel für einen Mann, der sich seine Aufträge nicht nur als junger Architekt, sondern auch später durch überlegene Wettbewerbsprojekte erkämpft hat, die er in den jüngeren Jahren in Zusammenarbeit mit anderen Architekten ausführte. Eines der ersten von Jacobsen gewonnenen Wettbewerbsprojekte war ein Vorschlag für das Bellevue-Bad in Klampenborg, der sich durch einen klaren und einfachen Lageplan auszeichnete. 1933 folgte die Wohnbebauung. Bellavista gegenüber dem Bad (Seite 28). Die dreiflügelige Anlage ist überlegen in das Gelände eingefügt. Versetzte Fassadenfluchten geben jeder einzelnen Wohnung Besonnung und gute Aussicht. Die Bebauung folgt in ihrem Äußeren den Gestaltungsprinzipien des internationalen Funktionalismus und ist wenigstens zum Teil mit den konstruktiven und technischen Widersprüchlichkeiten behaftet, die für diese Jahre unmittelbar nach 1930 typisch sind. Trotzdem wirkt die ganze Anlage sehr anmutig, und die Wohnungen sind nach wie vor stark gefragt.

1934-35 wurde die Bellevue-Bebauung mit dem Bellevue-Theater und einem damit verbundenen Restaurant fortgesetzt, womit Jacobsen einem wesentlichen Teil des alten Klampenborg eine neue Gestalt gab. Da das Theater hauptsächlich für Lustspiele und Revuen während der Sommersaison gedacht war, versuchte Jacobsen den Charme und die Leichtigkeit des Zirkuszeltes auf die neue Sommerbühne zu übertragen. Besonders reizvoll war die Wirkung, wenn das Schiebedach des Zuschauerraums zurückgefahren und der Sternenhimmel der Sommernächte sichtbar wurde. Leider zeigte sich nach einigen Jahren, daß weder das Theater noch das anschließende Restaurant rentabel waren aus Gründen, die der Architekt nicht zu vertreten hatte. Wechselnde Inhaber des Restaurants versuchten, mit Pappkulissen und schummrigen Beleuchtungseffekten eine Atmosphäre zu schaffen, die sie für Gemütlichkeit und Intimität hielten. Dabei wurde das Restaurant architektonisch verdorben, ohne daß es größeren Erfolg beim Publikum erzielt hätte. Später wurde es zu Reihenhauswohnungen umgebaut. Das Theater wurde in ein Kino umgewandelt und vermittelt in seiner jetzigen Gestalt nur noch einen schwachen Eindruck des ursprünglichen Baus, der eines der frischesten und reizvollsten Beispiele der dänischen Architektur in den dreißiger Jahren war.

Der Konflikt zwischen den ästhetisch aufgefaßten Architekturidealen, den technischen Möglichkeiten dieser Zeit und der Rücksicht auf das dänische Klima, die gebräuchlichen dänischen Baustoffe und die

restaurant were economically viable. By means of cardboard screens and dimmed lighting, successive restaurant proprietors tried to create an atmosphere which they regarded as congenial and intimate. The restaurant was thereby spoiled architecturally without, however, achieving any greater success with the public. Later, it was converted into terrace houses whilst the theatre was converted into a cinema and is, in its present form, no more than a weak reflection of the original building which was one of the freshest and most attractive examples of Danish architecture in the 1930's.

In due course, the conflict of the aesthetically conceived architectural ideas and technical potentialities of the time with considerations for the Danish climate and for traditional Danish building materials and workmanship enabled Arne Jacobsen to gather a good deal of useful experience. Having learned his lesson, he endeavoured, in the years that followed, to find a greater harmony between design and construction, and also to make greater use of traditional Danish building materials. He succeeded, for example, in avoiding the awkward maintenance problems encountered with white-washed concrete surfaces. In 1934-35, he built a tennis hall for Hellerup Sports Club (page 80) where the concrete arches are covered with roof felting. The roof reaches down right to the ground; end walls and the changing rooms annex are built in yellow brick. The beauty of this harmonious building complex was further enhanced by covering the end walls with creepers.

In 1936, Arne Jacobsen won a design competition for the stadium of the City of Gentofte (page 81) which was, however, only built during the years 1941-42. This is an "unpretentious" and well-proportioned group of buildings of red brick, with asbestos cement roofs inclined at 30°. In this case, Jacobsen did not follow any new ideas but solved the task in a sober and workmanlike mood.

During 1934-35, Jacobsen also gained a reputation in industrial architecture by designing the Novo Therapeutical Laboratory (page XI), a simple white-washed building in reinforced concrete with regularly spaced windows and a small garden. At the time, it was by no means usual, as yet, to create such a friendly and congenial environment for the staff of an industrial undertaking. One of his masterpieces was the petrol station at Skovshoved Harbour (page XI), erected in 1936-37 — a task which, at that time, was still regarded as being outside the normal sphere of activities and interest of architects. The elegant little building has a circular concrete roof which rests

Novo Terapeutiske Laboratorium, Kopenhagen, 1934-35.
Novo Therapeutical Laboratory, Copenhagen, 1934-35.

Tankstelle bei Skovshoved Havn, 1936.
Petrol filling station near Skovshoved Havn, 1936.

handwerklichen Traditionen hatte Arne Jacobsen nach und nach zu einer Reihe nützlicher Erfahrungen geführt. Aus Schaden klug geworden, suchte er in den folgenden Jahren eine bessere Übereinstimmung zwischen Gestaltung und Konstruktion zu finden und auch in größerem Umfang traditionelle dänische Baumaterialien zu verwenden. So ließen sich beispielsweise die großen Instandhaltungsprobleme der weiß gekalkten Betonoberflächen vermeiden. 1934-35 baute er eine Tennishalle für den Sportklub Hellerup (Seite 80), bei der Betonbogen mit Dachpappe überdeckt sind. Das Dach reicht bis zum Erdboden, die Stirnwände und der Bau mit den Umkleideräumen sind aus gelben Backsteinen gemauert. Die harmonische Baugruppe wurde in der Schönheit ihres Materials noch durch Kletterpflanzen an den Stirnwänden ergänzt.

1936 gewann Arne Jacobsen einen Wettbewerb für das Stadion der Gemeinde Gentofte (Seite 81), das aber erst in den Jahren 1941-42 gebaut wurde. Es ist eine bescheidene und wohlproportionierte Anlage von Bauten aus roten Steinen mit Eternitdächern von 30 Grad Neigung. Jacobsen ging hier keine neuen Wege, sondern löste die Aufgabe in nüchterner, handwerksgerechter Gesinnung.

Auch im Industriebau wurde Jacobsen 1934-35 durch das Novo Terapeutiske Laboratorium bekannt (Seite XI), ein einfacher weiß gekalkter Bau in Stahlbeton mit regelmäßiger Anordnung der Fenster und einer kleinen Gartenanlage. In jenen Jahren war es durchaus noch nicht üblich, für die Belegschaft eines industriellen Unternehmens eine so freundliche und wohltuende Umgebung zu schaffen. Ein Meisterstück wurde die 1936-37 errichtete Tankstelle bei Skovshoved Havn (Seite XI), eine Aufgabe, die zu diesem Zeitpunkt sonst außerhalb des Arbeitsgebietes und zumeist auch des Interesses der Architekten lag. Der elegante kleine Bau hat ein kreisrundes, schützendes Betondach, das durch einen breiten Steg mit dem dahinterliegenden kubischen Baukörper verbunden ist und auf einer Mittelstütze ruht. Die pilzförmige Stütze trägt auch die Beleuchtungskörper, deren nach oben gerichtetes Licht von der Unterseite des Daches reflektiert wird.

Schon während seiner Akademiezeit war Jacobsen in Stockholm Gunnar Asplund begegnet. Zwischen dem jungen vielversprechenden Studenten und dem zwanzig Jahre älteren Architekten hatte sich eine warme Freundschaft entwickelt, die durch den jährlich wiederkehrenden Besuch Jacobsens in der schwedischen Hauptstadt bis zu Asplunds viel zu frühem Tod im Jahre 1940 vertieft wurde. Daher konnte Jacobsen die Entstehung einiger Hauptwerke von Asplund genau verfolgen, wie des Warenhauses Bredenberg, das 1935 fertiggestellt wurde, des Rathauses von Göteborg, des staatlichen bakteriologischen Instituts von 1937 und des Waldkrematoriums von 1940. Alle diese Arbeiten sind durch einen klaren Entwurf und eine sowohl architektonisch wie auch handwerklich außerordentlich durchdachte Detaillierung geprägt.

Arne Jacobsen fühlte sich vor allem mit der Architekturauffassung und der disziplinierten Formsprache Asplunds verbunden, erkannte aber auch, wie schwach seine eigenen Arbeiten bei einem qualitativen Vergleich waren und wieviel er von Asplund lernen konnte. Wesentlich war vor allem, eine Aufgabe gründlich durchzuarbeiten und sie nicht eher abzuschließen, bevor nicht das kleinste Detail geklärt war. Und es war von Bedeutung, nicht nur jede Einzelheit sinngemäß zu gestalten, sondern sie auch dem gesamten Bild und der Bestimmung des Baues unterzuordnen.

Eines der Häuser, das besonders stark die Verbundenheit Jacobsens mit der Architektur Asplunds deutlich macht, wenn es sich auch als ein unverwechselbares Werk Arne Jacobsens ausweist, ist das Geschäftshaus Stelling am Gammeltorv in Kopenhagen (rechts). Die Beeinflussung wird vor allem in der Inneneinrichtung des Geschäfts

on a central column and is connected by a broad ribbon with the cubic building behind it. The mushroom-shaped column also carries the light fittings whose upward shining light is reflected by the underside of the roof.

During his Academy studies, Jacobsen has met Gunnar Asplund in Stockholm. Between the promising young student and the architect twenty years his senior, there developed a great friendship which was deepened by Jacobsen's regular annual visits to the Swedish capital until Asplund's far too early death in 1940. Jacobsen was therefore able to follow in detail the realisation of some of Asplund's major works such as the Bredenberg department stores which were completed in 1935, Gothenburg Town Hall, the State Bacteriological Institute (1937) and the Forest Crematorium (1940). All these works are distinguished by a clear design and by detailed planning which was, both architecturally and technically, extremely well considered. Arne Jacobsen felt particularly akin to Asplund's architectural outlook and his disciplined formal language; at the same time, he realised the comparative weakness of his own works, and how much he was able to learn from Asplund. The paramount requirement was to subject a task to thorough consideration, and not to conclude it before even the smallest detail had been clarified. Moreover, it was important that each detail should be designed not only in keeping with its own purpose but also in such a way that it was subordinated to the overall picture and to the raison d'être of the building.

Geschäftshaus A. Stelling, Kopenhagen, 1937-38.
A. Stelling's Building, Copenhagen, 1937-38.

deutlich, bei der die einzelnen funktionellen Elemente nach Möglichkeit voneinander getrennt sind. So werden zum Beispiel die Zuleitungen direkt von der Wand her zu den Lampen unabhängig von der Aufhängung geführt. Ohne die Forderungen der neuen Architektur nach Präzision und Klarheit außer acht zu lassen, hat Jacobsen für die Außenwände wetterbeständigere Materialien gewählt anstelle des in so vielen früheren Arbeiten angewandten weißen Verputzes. Die Stahlbetonkonstruktion ist in den oberen Geschossen mit glasierten grauen Keramikfliesen verkleidet, während die beiden unteren Ladengeschosse mit grün gestrichenen Stahltafeln bedeckt sind. Der Bau liegt in einem alten Stadtteil und wurde damals wegen seines »pietätlosen Modernismus« kritisiert. Heute aber erkennt man, wie gut dieses Haus sich dem Maßstab der alten Bauten anpaßt und wie sehr es auch im Material den urbanen Charakter des Viertels respektiert.

Das sensible Verständnis Jacobsens für die Landschaft wurde zum erstenmal deutlich in dem Sommerhaus (Seite 2), das er 1937 für sich selbst bei Gudmindrup Lyng in einer weiträumigen Heide- und Dünenlandschaft baute. Der Grundriß ist unkonventionell, mit einem Wohnflügel, der auf einer Düne liegt und ihrer gekrümmten Form folgt, während der Flügel mit den Schlafräumen am Fuß der Düne im Windschatten liegt. Eine interessante Raumwirkung entsteht durch den hochliegenden Aufenthaltsplatz mit seiner schönen Aussicht und dem tieferen Eßplatz, die durch eine Treppe miteinander verbunden sind, eine räumliche Anordnung, die später bei der Sø-

One of the houses which provides a particularly clear demonstration of Jacobsen's relationship with Asplund's architecture, though it is still unmistakably recognisable as Arne Jacobsen's work, is Stelling's House at Gammeltorv, Copenhagen (page XII). The influence is particularly obvious in the interior equipment of the shop where the different functional elements are, as far as possible, separated from each other. For example, the electric cables feeding the lamps are taken direct to them from the wall, independent of the suspension. Without disregarding the demands of modern architecture in respect of precision and clarity, Jacobsen chose, for the outer walls, materials of higher weathering resistance than the white plaster rendering which he had used in so many of his earlier works. The reinforced concrete structure is, in the upper storeys, clad with glazed grey ceramic tiles whilst the two lower floors, with the shop, are clad with steel plates painted green. The building is situated in an old part of the town and was, at the time, criticized for its "irreverent modernism." To-day, however, it is possible to appreciate how well this house measures up to the scale of the old buildings, and how much even its building material is in keeping with the congenial atmosphere of the district.

Jacobsen's sensitive understandling for landscape became first apparent with the summer cottage (page 2) which he built for himself in 1937 at Gudmindrup Lyng in a wide-open setting of heath and dunes. The plan is unorthodox, with a living room wing which is placed on one of the dunes and follows its curved shape whilst the

Haus Thorvald Pedersen, Klampenborg, 1938. Außen- und Innenansicht.
Thorvald Pedersen's House, Klampenborg, 1938.
Exterior and detail of Interior.

holm-Bebauung wiederkehrt. Alte Mühlsteine im Garten und eine Holzrampe an der Außenseite verleihen dem Haus einen robusten Charakter, der in der Architektur Arne Jacobsens ungewöhnlich ist.

Mit wenigen Jahren Abstand gewann Arne Jacobsen zwei große Rathaus-Wettbewerbe. Beim Rathaus von Århus (Seite 86) hatte er Erik Møller als Kompagnon. Das Projekt von 1937 war eine neuartige Lösung für kommunale Verwaltungsbauten. Die klare und funktionelle Anlage besteht aus einem Hauptflügel, an dessen Fassade sich der Ratssaal und die Halle durch die großen Fensterpartien deutlich abzeichnen, und einem längeren Büroflügel mit regelmäßig gegliederter Fassade. Das Projekt löste sofort nach dem Abschluß des Wettbewerbs heftige Kritik aus. Die Bürger der Stadt fanden, daß der Bau nicht die konventionelle Monumentalität zeigte, die sie sich bei einem Rathaus vorstellten. »Ein dänisches Rathaus sollte zu allererst in heimatlichem, dänischem Stein ausgeführt werden«, hieß es, »und im übrigen müßte es einen Turm haben.« Die Architekten kämpften lange dagegen an. Schließlich konnten sie das Projekt in seiner geplanten Form und mit dem vorgesehenen Material ausführen, mußten sich aber der Forderung nach einem Turm beugen. Die Lösung war nicht ungekonnt, schadete aber trotzdem der Gesamtanlage, denn der Turm wirkt wie ein angeklebtes, dekoratives Element ohne homogenen oder konstruktiven Zusammenhang mit dem sonst nüchternen Bau. Das Äußere des Gebäudes ist würdig und seiner Umgebung gut angepaßt, mit einer schönen Beziehung zwischen den Fenstern der Rathaushalle und den großen Bäumen davor. Die Halle selbst ist mit ihren Balkongalerien von konstruktiver Eleganz, jedoch wird der leichte Charakter des Raumes leider durch allzu gewichtige Beleuchtungskörper und eine dekorative Ausschmückung durch den Maler Hagedorn-Olsen teilweise wieder aufgehoben. Die Architekten können jedoch nicht für die Anbringung dieser der Architektur so fremden Malerei verantwortlich gemacht werden.

Als Arne Jacobsen mit Flemming Lassen als Partner drei Jahre später den Wettbewerb für das Rathaus in Søllerød (Seite 88) gewann, lag der Streit von Århus schon in weiter Ferne, so daß die meisten die Unsinnigkeit der Turm-Aktion einsahen. Auch beim Søllerød-Projekt mußten natürlich einige Schwierigkeiten überwunden werden, aber die Ausführung folgte doch recht genau dem Wettbewerbsvorschlag. Die Gemeinde Søllerød liegt in einem der waldreichsten Gebiete der Kopenhagener Umgebung und besteht hauptsächlich aus Villenvierteln. Das Rathaus erhielt denn auch einen besonders charakteristischen und schönen Platz nahe am Wald; die Nordseite ist der Stadt zugewandt. Das schlichte und würdige Bauwerk ist nur drei Geschosse hoch. Die sandgestrahlte Marmorbekleidung läßt es durch die Bäume des Waldes hindurch fast unwirklich erscheinen, als wenn es eine der Skizzen Jacobsens in ihren kühlen, grauweißen Tönen wäre. Die raffinierte Behandlung der Details im Inneren läßt an Asplunds Göteborger Rathaus denken, aber trotz dieses Vorbildes zeigen Möbel, Beschläge, Türgriffe und so weiter die persönliche Prägung Jacobsens und Lassens. Auch der Ratssaal ist ein außerordentlich schöner und selbständiger Raum.

Diese beiden Rathäuser bilden einen glücklichen Abschluß des dänischen Funktionalismus der dreißiger Jahre. Neue Materialien und Konstruktionen haben eine harmonische und natürliche Anwendung gefunden. Der Krieg brachte umfangreiche Materialeinschränkungen und Importverbote mit sich. Der heimische Backstein kam wieder zu Ehren. Gleichzeitig änderten sich die architektonischen Vorstellungen. Viele Architekten versuchten aus der Not eine Tugend zu machen und dabei die traditionellen Qualitäten von Handwerk und Material wieder aufleben zu lassen. Die Besatzung stärkte die nationalen Bestrebungen einer rein dänischen Kunst und unterstützte

bedroom wing lies wind-protected at the bottom of the dune. An interesting space effect is obtained by the high-level lounge with its beautiful view, and the dining place at a lower level connected with the lounge by stairs — an arrangement which is later again encountered at the Søholm estate. With some old millstones in the garden and a wooden ramp on the outside, the house has a robust character which is unusual in Arne Jacobsen's architecture.

Within a few years, Arne Jacobsen won two important competitions for town hall designs. With the town hall for Århus (page 86), he was partnered by Eric Møller. The 1937 project represented a novel solution for municipal administration buildings. The tidily arranged, functional group of buildings consists of a main block where the Council Chamber and the great hall are clearly marked by the large windows, and a longish office block with regularly partitioned façade. The project at once gave rise to violent criticism. The citizens found that the building did not show the conventional monumentality which they looked for in a town hall. "A Danish town hall should, first of all, be erected in native Danish stone," so they said, "and should in any case have a tower." For a long time, the architects objected. Eventually, they were allowed to carry out the project as designed, and with the material envisaged, but they had to comply with the demand for a tower. The solution was not without architectural merit; but is was detrimental to the group as a whole since the tower has the appearance of a stuck-on decorative element without any homogeneous or structural relationship to the otherwise sober building. The exterior of the building is dignified and well adapted to its surroundings, with a fine relationship between the town hall windows and the large trees in front of them. The hall itself, with its galleries, is structurally elegant; but the impression of lightness is unfortunately somewhat impaired by the unduly heavy light fittings and by decorations by the painter Hagedorn-Olsen. However, the architects cannot be held responsible for the application of this paintwork, so alien to the architectural design.

When, three years later, Arne Jacobsen in partnership with Flemming Lassen won the competition for Søllerød Town Hall (page 88), the Århus controversy was already so far removed that most people had come to see the senselessness of the tower campaign. Even with the Søllerød project, it was of course necessary to overcome some difficulties, but in the event, the building was erected in fairly good agreement with the original design. The Borough of Søllerød is situated in one of the most wooded areas in the vicinity of Copenhagen and consists mainly of smart detached houses. The town hall was therefore also allotted a particularly attractive and characteristic site near the woods; its North side faces the town. The unpretentious and dignified building has only three storeys. With its sand-blasted marble cladding, the building appears almost unreal through the trees of the wood, as if it were one of Jacobsen's sketches in their cool grey-white colour shades. The refined treatment of the interior details is reminiscent of Asplund's town hall at Gothenburg; but in spite of that example, Jacobsen's and Lassen's personal touch is apparent in the furniture, fittings, door handles etc. The Council Chamber, too, is an extremely attractive room of independent design.

These two town halls represent a felicitous climax to the Danish functionalism of the 1930's. New materials and new structural concepts found a harmonious and natural application. The War brought in its wake extensive import restrictions and shortages of materials. Native brick again came into its own. At the same time, there was a change in architectural thought. Many architects tried to make a virtue out of necessity, seeking to revive the traditional qualities of workmanship and material. The Occupation stimulated the national

damit eine Reaktion gegen den »sterilen, unpersönlichen und internationalen Modernismus« der dreißiger Jahre, den manche noch immer für unvereinbar mit dem Klima und der Mentalität Dänemarks hielten. So brachten die Kriegsjahre eine empfindliche Unterbrechung der natürlichen architektonischen Entwicklung mit sich.

Arne Jacobsen beschäftigte sich während der ersten Kriegsjahre hauptsächlich mit dem Wohnungsbau. Bei einigen Wohnblöcken in der Gemeinde Gentofte führten Bestimmungen für ausgebaute Dachetagen über zwei Wohngeschossen zu einer ungewöhnlichen Gestaltung. In der Wohnbebauung Ibstrupparken (Seite 36) von 1940 durchbrechen die Balkonerker das hohe Dach und verleihen mit ihrer rhythmischen Wiederholung den langen Trakten, die auf einer Böschung über der Autobahn nach Hørsholm liegen, eine besondere Note.

Die Materialbeschaffung wurde ständig schwieriger, besonders Stahl war kaum zu bekommen. Die Fensteröffnungen mußten deshalb so klein gehalten werden, daß sie mit einem gemauerten Sturz überdeckt werden konnten. Die Kettenhäuser am Ellebæksvej wurden deshalb in der traditionellen dänischen Bauweise errichtet. Es sind einzelstehende Einfamilienhäuser mit Erd- und Dachgeschoß, verbunden durch niedrige Zwischenbauten, die einen Abstellraum, Fahrradschuppen und so weiter enthalten. Diese zusammenhängende Bebauungsform wurde in jenen Jahren für viele Wohngebiete im ganzen Land zum Vorbild.

Die bedeutendste Arbeit Arne Jacobsens in dieser Periode war eine Heringsräucherei bei Odden Havn (Seite 17) auf Sjællands Odde. Inspiriert von alten Heringsräuchereien auf Bornholm, gelang es ihm, dem Bau ein markantes, fast monumentales Aussehen zu geben.

1943 wurde Arne Jacobsen durch die Umstände gezwungen, das besetzte Dänemark zu verlassen und nach Schweden zu flüchten, wo er sehr herzlich empfangen wurde. Er verbrachte dort fast zwei Jahre unter zwar bescheidenen, aber den Verhältnissen nach guten Arbeitsbedingungen. Schwedische Kollegen verschafften ihm zu Anfang Projektierungsaufträge beim Architekturbüro der schwedischen Wohnbaugesellschaft HSB. Gleichzeitig begann Jacobsen Stoff- und Tapetenmuster zu entwerfen. Seine große Fertigkeit im Zeichnen und seine kompositionelle Begabung kamen in diesen Arbeiten zum Ausdruck, die Motive aus der Vegetation der Grabenränder, der Wiesen und des Waldbodens aufgriffen. Zusammen mit seiner Frau, Jonna Jacobsen, die gelernte Stoffdruckerin war, führte er diese Entwürfe aus, die bald großen Erfolg hatten. Die Stoffe wurden vom Nationalmuseum in Stockholm angekauft, und große Textilfirmen begannen mit der Produktion. Auch beim Publikum fanden die Muster großen Anklang. Jacobsens Stoffe und Tapeten wurden noch lange nach dem Krieg sowohl in Schweden als auch in Dänemark verwendet, bis die architektonische Entwicklung wieder schlichte, einfarbige Wände forderte.

Als Arne Jacobsen 1945 von Schweden zurückkehrte, war die Arbeit seines Büros fast zum Stillstand gekommen. Die Bautätigkeit in Dänemark war natürlich stark reduziert, und strenge Einschränkungen bestanden noch einige Jahre lang. Jacobsen nutzte die Wartezeit mit der Beteiligung an vielen Wettbewerben. Dabei erhielt er zwei erste Preise für Projekte, die nie verwirklicht wurden: der eine 1946 in Gemeinschaft mit Nils Koppel für einen Waldpavillon in Hobro, der andere 1949 für einen Jachthafen mit Restaurant in Vejle (Seite 82). 1948 erhielt er den zweiten Preis für einen Vorschlag zum Neubau der Handels- og Kontoristforening in Kopenhagen. Außerdem hatte er in mehreren anderen Wettbewerben Erfolg mit Entwürfen, die nicht zuletzt auch von seiner hervorragenden Darstellungstechnik mit virtuos ausgeführten, farbigen Perspektiven geprägt

tendencies for purely Danish art and thereby supported a reaction against the "sterile, impersonal and international modernism" of the 1930's which was still regarded, by some, as incompatible with Danish climate and mentality. The war years thus caused a marked interruption of the natural architectural development.

During the first years of the War, Arne Jacobsen was mainly concerned with housing construction. In the case of some blocks of flats in the City of Gentofte, the building regulations concerning mansard roofs above two storeys gave rise to an unusual design. At the Ibstrupparken housing estate (page 36) of 1940, situated on a slope above the Hørsholm Motorway, the balcony alcoves penetrate the high roof and form, with their rhythmic repetition, a characteristic feature of the long blocks.

At that time, the shortage of building materials became more and more acute and steel, in particular, was hardly available. It was therefore necessary to keep the window openings so small that they could be covered by brick heads. The chain-type houses at Ellebæksvej were therefore erected in the traditional Danish style. They are one-family houses with ground floor and attic, connected by low annexes which contain a store room, bicycle shed, etc. This coherent type of housing became, in those years, an example for many housing estates throughout the country.

Arne Jacobsen's most important work during that period was a herring smoking plant at Odden Havn (page 17) on the peninsula known as Sjællands Odde. Inspired by some old plants of this kind which he had encountered in the Island of Bornholm, he succeeded in giving this building a characteristic and almost monumental appearance.

In 1943, Arne Jacobsen was forced by political circumstances to leave occupied Denmark and to take refuge in Sweden where he was cordially welcomed. There he spent nearly two years under modest, but in the circumstances, good working conditions. At first, with the assistance of Swedish colleagues, he was commissioned to prepare designs for the architectural office of the Swedish housing association "H.S.B." At the same time, Jacobsen began to design textile and wallpaper patterns. These designs, using motifs from the wild flora of ditches, meadows and woods, showed up his great drawing skill and his talent for composition. Together with his wife, Jonna Jacobsen, who was a trained textile printer, he put these designs into practice; they soon met with great success. The materials were acquired by the National Museum, Stockholm, and textile firms began production. With the public, too, the patterns became very popular. Even long after the War, Jacobsen's materials and wallpapers were still used both in Sweden and in Denmark until the architectural trend again called for more anonymous, single-coloured walls.

When, in 1945, Arne Jacobsen returned from Sweden, the work of his office had virtually come to a standstill. At that time, building activities in Denmark were of course greatly reduced, and severe restrictions persisted for some years. Jacobsen made use of the enforced waiting time by taking part in many competitions. During that period, he won two First Prizes for projects which never materialized: one in 1946, in cooperation with Nils Koppel, for a forest pavilion at Hobro; the other in 1949 for a yacht harbour with restaurant at Vejle (page 82). In 1948, he won the Second Prize for a project for a new headquarters building of the "Handels- od Kontoristforening" in Copenhagen. He was also successful with designs for several other competitions which were also distinguished by the excellent manner of presentation, with brilliantly executed coloured perspectives. But in spite of the lucidity and skill which they reflect, these projects may perhaps be regarded as being among Jacob-

waren. Diese Projekte, so klar und gekonnt sie auch durchgestaltet waren, gehören trotzdem wohl zu Jacobsens weniger bedeutungsvollen Arbeiten. Wie bei vielen anderen Architekten war auch in Jacobsens Werk Unsicherheit gegenüber einer neuen Zeit spürbar, in der man nicht mehr allein auf die traditionellen Materialien und Konstruktionen angewiesen war, sondern sich wieder Inspirationen von draußen holen und eine Formensprache suchen konnte, die mehr im Einklang mit der technischen und künstlerischen Entwicklung war.

Eine schöne Arbeit dieser Nachkriegsjahre sind die Wohnbauten für junge Ehepaare in Gentofte, 1947 (Seite 38). Keiner sollte hier länger als fünf Jahre wohnen, so daß die kleinen Wohnungen nur jungen Familien mit niedrigem Einkommen vorbehalten blieben und im Laufe der Zeit keine Überbelegung zu befürchten war. Die dreigeschossigen Wohnblöcke aus gelbem Backstein lagen ursprünglich zwischen hohen Bäumen an einem kleinen See, der nun zugeschüttet ist. Die Anlage erweist sich aber auch jetzt noch als eine der gelungensten Wohnbebauungen Arne Jacobsens mit ihrem freundlichen, zwanglosen Charakter und dem lebhaften Spiel der hohen und niedrigen geschlossenen Giebel längs der Straßenböschung.

Entscheidend für die Wiedererringung seiner Position in der dänischen Architektur war Jacobsens Søholm-Bebauung (Seite 40) bei Bellevue, deren erster Bauabschnitt 1950 fertiggestellt wurde. Aufgabe war, an Stelle eines schön gelegenen Landhauses, das niedergerissen wurde, einer größtmöglichen Anzahl von Häusern hoher Wohnqualität gleichen Anteil an der Aussicht auf das Meer zu geben. Die Lösung ist ganz untraditionell und erinnert an südeuropäische, anonyme ländliche Architektur mit schmalen zweigeschossigen, gegeneinander versetzten Hauskörpern und unsymmetrischen Dachformen. Die plastische Wirkung dieser Baukörper ist kräftiger und lebendiger als sonst bei Jacobsen. Formal am gelungensten sind die nach Südosten orientierten Häuser, die nicht nur die besten Aussichtsmöglichkeiten haben, sondern auch am engsten mit dem eigenen Garten verbunden sind. Der Blick über den Øresund und die sonnige Terrasse verleihen diesen Wohnungen einen besonderen Reiz. Arne Jacobsen selbst wohnt in dem Haus, das dem Wasser am nächsten liegt und größer als die übrigen ist. Besonders ein zusätzlicher Raum im ersten Stock gibt dem Wohnbereich eine schöne räumliche Erweiterung. Der Garten vor dem Haus ist fast ein Märchen. Auf einem Minimum an Fläche wachsen nahezu tausend verschiedene Pflanzenarten. Hier experimentiert Jacobsen mit dänischen und ausländischen Gewächsen und sammelt nützliche Erfahrungen für die Garten- und Landschaftsgestaltung, die ihm so sehr am Herzen liegt.

Die Westhäuser dagegen haben gewisse Schwächen im Grundriß, und es fehlt ihnen der restlos überzeugende Zusammenklang zwischen der äußeren Form, dem konstruktiven Aufbau und der räumlichen Gestaltung im Inneren. Zusammen mit den 1955 hinzugekommenen eingeschossigen Bauten ordnen sie sich jedoch sehr glücklich in die Gesamtanlage ein, die eine der reizvollsten im modernen dänischen Wohnbau ist.

Die Strandvejsbugt bei Bellevue ist von Arne Jacobsen ständig stärker geprägt worden. Zuletzt kam 1960-61 eine Bebauung hinzu (Seite 50), die sich direkt an das alte Bellavista anschließt. Wie in Søholm war die Aufgabe gestellt, möglichst viele Luxuswohnungen mit Aussicht über den Sund auf begrenzter Fläche unterzubringen. Das Ergebnis war ein über 20 m tiefer, viergeschossiger Wohnblock an der Westseite des Grundstücks mit schmalen, aber in ganzer Tiefe durchgehenden Wohnungen und davor, zum Sund hin gelegen, fünf große eingeschossige Atriumhäuser. Über diese Anordnung kann man geteilter Meinung sein, weil der Blick der höher liegenden

sen's less significant works. As with many other architects, Jacobsen's works, too, showed traces of uncertainty when confronted with a new era in which it was no longer necessary exclusively to rely on traditional materials and structural concepts and in which it was again possible to derive inspiration from abroad and to seek a formal language more in keeping with technical and artistic trends. A fine work dating from these post-war years is the housing estate for young married couples at Gentofte, built in 1947 (page 38). The idea was that no-one should stay here longer than five years so that the small flats would always be reserved for young couples with low incomes, and so that there would be no excessive demand for the flats in the course of time. The three-storey blocks of yellow brick were originally situated between high trees at the side of a small lake which has meanwhile been filled in. But even now, the buildings still represent one of the most successful housing ventures designed by Arne Jacobsen, with their friendly and informal character and the vivid play of the high and low gables along the road embankment.

Decisive for his recapture of a leading position among Danish architects was Jacobsen's Søholm housing estate (p. 40) near Bellevue where the first buildings were completed in 1950. The task was that of replacing a beautifully situated villa, which bad been demolished, by the greatest possible number of high-class houses where each was to be given a fair share of the sea view. The solution adopted by Jacobsen is quite unorthodox, and is reminiscent of anonymous rural Mediterranean architecture with narrow two-storey blocks in staggered position and with non-symmetric roof shapes. The plastic effect of this group of buildings is stronger and more vivid than is usually the case with Jacobsen. Perhaps the most successful design is that of the houses facing South-East which not only have the best view but are also most closely conjoined with their own gardens. With their view across the Sound and their sunny terrace, these dwellings are particularly attractive. Arne Jacobsen himself lives in the house nearest to the sea, which is somewhat larger than the rest. In particular, an additional room on the first floor forms an attractive extension of the living space. The front garden is of almost fairy-tale luxuriance. On an area of minimum size, there grow nearly a thousand different species of plants. Here, Jacobsen is experimenting with Danish and foreign plants and is collecting useful experience for the type of landscape gardening which is so close to his heart.

In contrast, the houses on the West side have certain weaknesses in the plan, and they lack a fully convincing cohesion between external design, structure, and internal layout. However, together with the single-storey buildings which were added in 1955, they are felicitously in keeping with the entire building complex which now represents one of the most attractive compositions in modern Danish housing. The bay skirted by the coastal road near Bellevue, Klampenborg, has more and more come to bear Jacobsen's hallmark. The latest addition came in 1960-61 in the form of a housing estate (page 50) which is in direct connection with the old Bellavista estate. As in the case of Søholm, the task was to accommodate, on a strictly limited area, as many luxury dwellings as possible, with a view across the Sound. The result was a four-storey block of more than 20 metres depth on the West side of the plot, with narrow dwellings extending through the whole depth of the building and, in front of this block facing the Sound, five large-single-storey atrium houses. One may have different opinions about this arrangement, since the view from the upper-storey dwellings ranges over the extensive flat roofs of the atrium houses; even so, these dwellings with their wide balconies and large roof terraces in the top

Wohnungen auf die ausgedehnten flachen Dächer der Einfamilienhäuser fällt, aber dennoch sind diese Wohnungen mit ihren breiten Balkonen und den großen Dachterrassen im obersten Geschoß sehr attraktiv. Die Einfamilienhäuser haben ein Aussichtsfenster nach Osten zum Sund hin, die Wohnräume sind jedoch auf den inneren Hofraum hin orientiert.

1946 wurde die Ibstrup-Bebauung am Smakkegårdsvej mit einigen einfachen, dreigeschossigen Zeilen aus gelbem Backsteinmauerwerk — Wohnbauten für gehobene Ansprüche — fortgesetzt (Seite 37). 1952 kamen neue dreigeschossige Wohnblöcke an der Jægersborg Allé hinzu (Seite 47). Bei diesen letzteren Bauten sind die versetzten Loggien und die mansardenähnlichen Dachdurchbrechungen besonders bemerkenswert. Diese Anordnung der Loggien hat zwar den Vorteil einer besseren Abschirmung gegeneinander, bringt aber auch Schwierigkeiten im Grundriß und in der Belichtung der Räume mit sich. Solange die Bauten noch frei standen, behaupteten sie sich durch ihre plastische Wirkung. Sie werden nun aber empfindlich beeinträchtigt, nachdem sie 1957 von neuen Flügeln eingeschlossen wurden, die im Gegensatz zu der früheren Bebauung glatte Fassaden ohne Balkons haben. Es ist Jacobsen hier nicht recht geglückt, die verschiedenen Baukörper zu einer Einheit zusammenzuschließen. Als alleiniger Architekt hätte er die Möglichkeit dazu gehabt, selbst wenn die Gesamtanlage in einem Zeitraum von zwanzig Jahren entstanden ist. Auch die Freiräume zwischen den Bauten sind an vielen Stellen unklar. Es scheint, daß hier die Experimentierlust Jacobsens stärker war als die Bemühung um einen geschlossenen Gesamteindruck.

Daß Arne Jacobsen auch für Leute mit geringerem Einkommen zu bauen vermag, bewies er mit der Reihenhaussiedlung Islevvænge in Rødovre (Seite 46). Hier bilden einfache, vernünftige Häuser aus gelbem Backstein eine schöne geschlossene Anlage um eine gemeinsame Grünfläche. Mit der gleichen Klarheit ist die Zentralschule in Hårby auf Fünen 1950 gestaltet (Seite 56). In der Größenordnung und der Auflösung in viele kleine Einheiten ist diese Schule den freistehenden, langgestreckten Häusern des dänischen Dorfes angepaßt und besticht durch ihre einfachen klaren Formen und Materialien.

Anfang der vierziger Jahre erfuhr der Schulbau in Dänemark eine entscheidende Wende. Die Reaktion gegen die monumentalen Schulanlagen der zwanziger und dreißiger Jahre kam zum Durchbruch. Architekten und moderne Pädagogen forderten eine freundlichere Atmosphäre für die Kinder und Schulen von einer Größenordnung, die mehr Rücksicht auf die Kleinen nahm, auch auf Kosten verwaltungstechnischer Vorteile für Schulleiter und Lehrer. Es entstanden mehrere interessante Wettbewerbsprojekte für eingeschossige Schulen, und einige davon wurden auch gleich nach dem Krieg verwirklicht. Die Munkegårds-Schule, erbaut 1952-56 (Seite 60), ist zwar nicht die erste ihrer Art, aber sie zeigt die bis jetzt klarste architektonische Lösung und zählt zu den Hauptwerken Arne Jacobsens. Bei der Gestaltung dieser Aufgabe verarbeitete Jacobsen Inspirationen aus dem Ausland zu einem Werk von überragender Bedeutung.

Das Grundstück und die häßlichen Häuser in nächster Umgebung schlossen eine offene Anlage mit grünen Gartenflächen zwischen freiliegenden Baukörpern aus, die an vielen anderen Orten richtig gewesen wäre. Dagegen war hier eine nach innen gerichtete, in sich geschlossene Lösung wohlbegründet. Der regelmäßige Wechsel von Normalklassen und Gartenhöfen ergab einen übersichtlichen Lageplan. Die paarweise angeordneten Klassenräume, an die jeweils ein Vorraum mit Garderobe anschließt, sind durch helle und freundliche Korridore miteinander verbunden. Aula und Lehrerzimmer sind

floor are highly attractive. The single-family houses have a picture window facing the Sound on the East side, but the living rooms face the inner courtyard.

In 1946, the Ibstrup housing estate at Smakkegårdsvej was extended by some rows of simple three-storey blocks of high-class flats, erected in yellow brick (page 37). In 1952, some new three-storey blocks were added, facing Jægersborg Allé (page 47). With these latter buildings, the staggered loggias and the mansard-like roof penetrations are particularly interesting features. Whilst this arrangement of the loggias has the advantage of greater privacy, it also gives rise to certain difficulties in the plan and in the daylighting of the rooms. As long as the buildings were still standing in isolation, they asserted themselves through their sheer plastic effect. Since 1957, however, when they were enclosed by new buildings which in contrast to the earlier ones had smooth facades without balconies, the effect of the older buildings is somewhat impaired. Here, Jacobsen has not been quite successful in combining the different blocks into an integrated whole. As the sole architect in charge, he would have had the facilities even though the whole complex of buildings was built over a period of 20 years. Even the open spaces between the buildings are, at many points, unconvincing. It would seem that in this case, Jacobsen's predilection for experiments was stronger than his endeavour to create an integrated overall impression.

That Arne Jacobsen is also able to build for clients in the lower income groups, he proved with his design for the Islevvænge terrace house estate in Rødovre (page 46). Here, some simple and sensible houses of yellow brick form an attractive enclosed group around a communal open space. Similar lucidity distinguishes the Central School at Hårby on the island of Funen, built in 1950 (page 56). In its general scale, and with its division into many small units, this school blends well with the self-contained oblong houses traditionally encountered in Danish villages; its simple and clear shapes and materials are attractive.

During the early 1940's, Danish school architecture took a decisive turn. The reaction against monumental school buildings of the 1920's and 1930's was in full swing. Architects and modern pedagogues insisted on a friendlier atmosphere for the children, and called for schools on a scale more in keeping with the children, even — if necessary — at the expense of administrative advantages to headmaster and teachers. This gave rise to several interesting competition projects for bungalow type schools, and some of them were in fact realised just after the War. Munkegårds School, built in 1952-56 (page 60), is admittedly not the first of its kind; but it is distinguished by the most lucid architectural solution adopted so far, and must be counted among Arne Jacobsen's principal works. In tackling this task, Jacobsen was able to make use of inspirations from abroad and to distil them into a work of outstanding importance.

Because of the shape of the site and the ugly houses in its immediate vicinity, a loose group of isolated buildings embedded in green — a solution which would have been right in many other places — had to be ruled out. But there were sound reasons for adopting a solution which provided for a self-contained group of inwards oriented buildings. The regular alternation between standard classrooms and patios gave rise to a tidy layout plan. The classrooms, arranged in pairs and combined with ante-rooms and cloak-rooms of their own, are linked by bright and friendly corridors. Assembly hall and staffrooms are comprised in the patio system in the same organic manner as the two-storey block with special classrooms which forms the rear end of the group of buildings.

The numerous patios are clearly distinguished from each other by the type of flags and vegetation used. Each of them is decorated

ebenso organisch in das Gartenhofsystem einbezogen wie der zweigeschossige Trakt mit den Spezialklassen, der den hinteren Abschluß der Anlage bildet.

Die vielen Gartenhöfe sind durch die Art des Bodenbelags und der Bepflanzung sehr verschieden gestaltet. In jedem Hof steht als besonderer Schmuck der Abguß einer wertvollen Plastik und gibt ihm und damit auch den zugeordneten Normalklassen ein eigenes Gepräge. Darüber hinaus enthält der eine ein Bassin mit Wasserpflanzen, in einem zweiten blühen üppig wachsende Blumen, während in einem dritten die Büsche in Form von lustigen Tiergestalten geschnitten sind.

Die Details der Installationen und Beschläge sind mit der gleichen Sorgfalt gestaltet wie die Tische und Stühle der Normalklassen und das Inventar der Spezialklassen. Ursprünglich war der Einwand erhoben worden, daß die Schule zu wenig robust wäre und daß die Kinder sowohl die Bauten als auch die Bepflanzung bald ruiniert haben würden, aber nun, eine Reihe von Jahren nach der Fertigstellung, kann gesagt werden, daß das Gebäude sich bewährt hat und die Kinder die Schönheit der Anlage respektieren. Wenn auch die Schule in ihrer künstlerischen Gestaltung einen Höhepunkt im internationalen Schulbau darstellen mag, wirkt sie in ihrer Konzeption doch nicht gewollt avantgardistisch; der erste Eindruck ist der einer intimen und menschlichen Atmosphäre.

Ein ähnlich freundliches Milieu wurde in der vor einiger Zeit eingeweihten Korsgårdens Børneinstitution (Kindergarten und Freizeitheim für Schüler) in Skovshoved geschaffen, die in einer etwas abgewandelten Form nach einem Projekt von 1949 ausgeführt wurde. Auch die Gemeindeschule in Rødovre (Seite 74) dürfte ein neuer Beweis für Jacobsens Fähigkeit werden, eine natürliche und schöne Umgebung für Kinder zu schaffen. Dieses Projekt ist nach einem mit dem ersten Preis ausgezeichneten Wettbewerbsentwurf von 1959 entstanden.

Nach der Isolation der Kriegsjahre wurden die USA das Land, von dem sich die dänischen Architekten die meisten Anregungen holten. Vor allem waren es Frank Lloyd Wright und Mies van der Rohe, deren Arbeiten zunächst in Zeitschriften und Büchern studiert wurden. Bei Wright bewunderte man die organische Einheit, die plastische Wirkung und die räumliche Konzeption seiner Bauten. Sein Einfluß wurde besonders beim dänischen Einfamilienhaus wirksam, vor allem in der freieren Grundrißgestaltung und der Einfügung in die Landschaft. Bei Mies beeindruckten die logische Schlichtheit seiner von der Konstruktion her entwickelten Architektur, die klassisch sichere Proportionierung nach einfachen geometrischen Regeln und die durchgearbeitete Detaillierung. Die Produktionsmethoden und die Präzisionsarbeit der Industrie wurden von Mies für die Architektur fruchtbar gemacht — in einer Qualität, die auf gleicher Höhe mit dem besten Handwerk lag.

Es war nur natürlich, daß Jacobsen bei seiner ganzen Mentalität und architektonischen Auffassung zu Mies tendierte. Er hat zwar dessen amerikanische Arbeiten nie gesehen, war aber mit den Gedanken und Werken von Mies selbstverständlich vertraut. Die Inspiration durch Mies van der Rohe führte zu einer schlichten, fast anonym bescheidenen Formensprache, die sich in Qualität und Verfeinerung seiner Arbeiten ausdrückte. Diese Züge stimmten zweifellos besser mit dänischen Traditionen und mit Jacobsens eigenen früheren Werken überein als Wrights geniale, aber stark gefühlsbetonte und von seiner eigenwilligen Persönlichkeit geprägte Architektur.

Die in den USA für den Büro- und Verwaltungsbau entwickelten Konstruktionen mit Curtain Walls fanden wie in vielen anderen Ländern auch in Dänemark große Verbreitung. Arne Jacobsen war

by the casting of a valuable sculpture which provides a distinguishing feature not only for the patio but also for the standard classrooms associated with it. Moreover, one of the patios has a pool of water with aquatic plants; another is distinguished by luxuriantly growing flowers; in a third, the shrubs are clipped so as to form gay shapes of animals.

Details of installations and fittings are designed with the same care as the tables and chairs of the standard classrooms and the furniture of the special classrooms. Originally, the objection was raised that the school was not robust enough and that the children would soon ruin not only the buildings but also the vegetation; now, however, after a number of years in service, it can be stated that the school has been a success and that the children have respected its beauty. Although the school, in its artistic design, may well be regarded as a crowning achievement in international school architecture, its concept does not suggest the deliberate adoption of an avant-garde design; the first impression is that of an intimate and human atmosphere.

A similarly friendly milieu has been created at the Korsgården Children's Institution (comprising a kindergarten and a spare-time home for school children) which was opened a short while ago at Skovshoved; the design dates back to a project of 1949 which was later somewhat modified. Similarly, the Council School at Rødovre (page 74) might be regarded as a renewed proof of Jacobsen's ability of creating natural and attractive environments for children. This design was based on a competition project which had been awarded a First Prize in 1959.

After the war-time isolation, it was to the United States that Danish architects turned so get most of their inspirations. In particular, it was the works of Frank Lloyd Wright and Mies van der Rohe which were studied, first of all, from journals and books. In Wright's work, one admired the organic unity, the plastic effect and the space conception. His influence in Denmark was particularly noticeable in the sphere of high-class detached houses, especially as regards the greater freedom in shaping the layout and the adaption of the house to the landscape. In Mies van der Rohe's works, the main objects of admiration were the logical unpretentiousness of his architecture based on technical considerations, his classically sure touch in choosing the proportions in accordance with simple geometrical rules, and his thorough attention to details. Mies van der Rohe had been able to utilise industrial production methods and precision work for the purposes of his architecture, and that on a level of quality in keeping with best workmanship.

It was only natural that Jacobsen, with his entire mentality and architectural thinking, tended to fall in with Mies van der Rohe. Though he has never seen the latter's American creations on the spot, he was of course familiar with Mies van der Rohe's ideas and works. The inspiration derived from him led to an unpretentious, almost anonymously modest formal language which was reflected in the quality and refinement of Jacobsen's works. These traits were undoubtedly in better agreement with Danish traditions and with Jacobsen's own earlier works than Wright's ingenious but rather emotional architecture which bears the imprint of the architect's own strong-willed personality.

As in many other countries, the curtain wall type of structure developed in the United States for office and administrative buildings also became popular in Denmark. Arne Jacobsen was one of the first to use this system in his country, and in any case the first to endow it with architectural quality. In the mid-1950's, three of such curtain wall structures came into being almost simultaneously: Glostrup Town Hall (page 102), Rødovre Town Hall (page 90), and the head-

einer der ersten, die hier dieses System anwandten — auf jeden Fall aber der erste, der ihm auch architektonische Qualität verlieh. In der Mitte der fünfziger Jahre entstanden fast gleichzeitig drei Projekte mit Curtain Walls: das Rathaus von Glostrup (Seite 102), das Rathaus von Rødovre (Seite 90) und der Verwaltungsbau der Firma Jespersen & Søn (Seite 117) in Kopenhagen.

Sogleich erhob sich von vielen Seiten starke Kritik gegen »diesen ganz unpersönlichen, menschenfeindlichen Internationalismus in Dänemark, wo die gute Bautradition mit ihrer alten Backsteintechnik und allenfalls auch noch die Stahlbetontechnik in einem Maße entwickelt war, daß kein Bedarf für diesen konstruktiven Modernismus bestand, der überall in der Welt gleich war«. Jacobsen selbst nahm die Kritik ruhig hin, und die Zeit hat ihm recht gegeben. Das Rathaus von Rødovre und das Bürohaus für Jespersen sind Bauten, die voll und ganz ihren Zweck erfüllen, wenn sie auch im technischen Detail einzelne Schwierigkeiten aufweisen, die sich bei neuen Konstruktionsprinzipien anfangs wohl nie ganz vermeiden lassen. Aber darüber hinaus hat Jacobsen auch den Sieg davongetragen, indem er die neue vereinfachte Formensprache zu seiner eigenen machte und jedem seiner Bauten eine persönliche Note verlieh.

Das Verwaltungsgebäude Jespersen & Søn (Seite 117) fügt sich trotz seiner individuellen Gestaltung gut in die Fassadenflucht der beiden benachbarten Gebäude ein. Der von der Konstruktion unabhängige Curtain Wall ist in Holz und Aluminium ausgeführt, die Eleganz des Baues wird unterstrichen durch das offene Erdgeschoß mit seinen Zufahrts- und Parkmöglichkeiten. Das Treppenhaus an der Schmalseite verleiht der Konstruktion die nötige Aussteifung. Durch diese Anordnung ergibt sich die größtmögliche zusammenhängende Geschoßfläche, die die günstigsten Voraussetzungen für die Aufstellung versetzbarer Trennwände bietet. Bei aller Einfachheit hat der Bau einen unverwechselbaren Charakter dank seiner feinen Proportionen und seiner gut gestalteten Details, wie zum Beispiel der ganz verglasten kleinen Wendeltreppe im offenen Erdgeschoß.

Das Rathaus von Rødovre (Seite 90) besteht aus zwei funktionell und räumlich klar getrennten Baukörpern, die rechtwinklig zueinander gestellt sind. Seine Würde als das vornehmste Haus der Gemeinde erhält der Bau teils durch seine freie Lage auf einer offenen großen Grünfläche, wo seine Fassaden durch die Spiegelung von Himmel und Wolken reich belebt werden, teils durch seine ausgewogenen Proportionen und die grauschwarze Marmorverkleidung an den Stirnwänden des Büroflügels und den Längsseiten des niedrigen Baukörpers. Das Äußere erinnert an das General Motors Center von Saarinen in Detroit. Im Inneren ist die Haupttreppe mit ihren Wangen aus Stahl und den Geländerfüllungen aus vorgespanntem Sicherheitsglas eine für Jacobsen charakteristische Arbeit. Die indirekte Beleuchtung des Ratssaales ist auf originelle Art gelöst, indem an abgehängten dünnen Rohren zahlreiche, gleichmäßig angeordnete kleine Zylinderlampen optisch eine tiefere Deckenebene bilden, die dem Raum besondere Intimität verleiht. Der Saal ist mit Möbeln nach eigenen Entwürfen Jacobsens ausgestattet, die gleichzeitig auch als Standardmodelle in den Handel kamen.

Den öffentlichen Wettbewerb für ein neues Rathaus in Glostrup (Seite 102) gewann Jacobsen 1953 mit einem Projekt, das sich durch einen klaren Grundriß auszeichnete und ein ähnliches Konstruktionsprinzip wie Rødovre hatte. Durch gemauerte Wandteile an Stirn- und Längsseiten sollte eine Beziehung zu der bestehenden älteren Bebauung um die benachbarte Kirche hergestellt werden. Leider fand Jacobsen nicht das gleiche Verständnis bei der Gemeinde, wie er es bei der Ausführung des Rathauses von Rødovre, der Munkegårds-Schule und bei anderen Projekten gefunden hatte. Zahlreiche Ände-

quarters building of Messrs. Jespersen & Søn (page 117) in Copenhagen.

At once, strong criticism was levelled from many sides against "this entirely impersonal, inhuman internationalism in Denmark where good building tradition with its ancient brick building technique and, for that matter, the reinforced concrete technique had already been developed to such a degree that there was no need for this structural modernism which was identical throughout the world." Jacobsen himself took the criticism calmly, and time has been on his side. Rødovre Town Hall and the Jespersen headquarters are buildings which fully meet the purposes for which they are designed, even if they still show certain difficulties in technical details which can presumably never be quite avoided where new design principles are tried out for the first time. But Jacobsen has also been successful in adopting the new simplified formal language as his own and endowing each of his buildings with a personal note.

In spite of its unorthodox design, the Jespersen headquarters building (page (117) is well in line with adjacent buildings. The curtain wall, which is independent of the bearing structure, is made of wood and aluminium, and the elegance of the building is emphasized by the open ground floor with its facilities for access and car parking. The staircase at the narrow side provides the necessary wind bracing. This arrangement yields the largest possible coherent floor area which offers the most favourable conditions for the use of mobile partitions. Despite all its simplicity, this building has an unmistakable character owing to its fine proportions and its well designed details, such as the small, entirely glazed spiral staircase in the open ground floor.

Rødovre Town Hall (page (90) consists of two functionally and physically separated blocks which stand at right angles to each other. The impression of dignity associated with the most representative building in the Borough stems partly from its isolated position in a wide open space where its facades are enlivened by the reflection of sky and clouds, and partly from the well-balanced proportions and the grey-black marble cladding of the front walls of the office wing and the long sides of the low block. The exterior is reminiscent of Saarinen's General Motors Center at Detroit. Inside, the main stairs with their stringers of steel and their side protection of prestressed safety glass are features characteristic for Jacobsen's work. The indirect lighting of the Council Chamber has found an original solution; it is provided by numerous, regularly spaced small cylindrical lights which are suspended in thin tubes and appear to form a second, lower ceiling, thus enhancing the intimacy of the room. The furniture of the Chamber is of Jacobsen's own design; it was, at the same time, series-produced for the commercial market.

The public competition for a new Town Hall at Glostrup (page 102) was won by Jacobsen in 1954 with a project which was distinguished by a clear layout and embodied a structural principle similar to that adopted for Rødovre. Through brick walls over parts of the short and long sides of the block, it was intended to create a link with the pre-existing older buildings around the adjacent church. Unfortunately, Jacobsen did not find the same understanding on the part of the local authorities as he had enjoyed in his design for Rødovre Town Hall, Munkegårds School and other projects. He was required to work out numerous alternatives; in particular, he was asked to provide a building which could be constructed in brick only. The final solution, adopted in 1959, was a compromise; a three-storey block with red brick pillars and continuous vertical windows. The building commands respect but does not occupy a specially high position among Jacobsen's other works.

This town hall project clearly shows the importance of the client's

rungsvorschläge mußten ausgearbeitet werden, so wurde unter anderem ein reiner Backsteinbau gefordert. Die endgültige Lösung von 1958 war ein Kompromiß, ein dreigeschossiger Bau mit roten Backsteinpfeilern und durchgehenden senkrechten Fensterpartien. Das Gebäude ist eine achtbare Leistung, nimmt aber unter den anderen Arbeiten Jacobsens keinen besonders hohen Rang ein.

An diesem Rathausprojekt wird deutlich, wie wichtig die Einstellung des Bauherrn ist. Zwar soll sich der Bauherr nicht den Launen des Architekten unterordnen, aber er soll doch, wenn er sein Programm formuliert hat, dem Architekten in diesem Rahmen eine gewisse Freiheit lassen. Wenn man sieht, wie konsequent Arne Jacobsen so viele seiner Bauten hat durchführen können, liegt der Schluß nahe, daß er ein Architekturdiktator war. Aber das stimmt nicht, er hat immer versucht, die Wünsche seiner Bauherren zu verstehen und zu verwirklichen, Wesentliches von Unwesentlichem zu unterscheiden und aus dieser Sicht seine Aufgaben zu lösen. Bei der weiteren Bearbeitung eines Projektes verlangt er nur, daß die Arbeit des Architekten respektiert wird, was bei seinem großen fachlichen Können durchaus begründet ist.

Die vorläufig letzte größere Arbeit im Bereich des sogenannten internationalen Konstruktivismus ist das Gebäude für die SAS (Scandinavian Airlines System, Seite 120) in Kopenhagen. Auch bei diesem Bau wird deutlich, daß sich Arne Jacobsen Anregungen aus den USA zu eigen gemacht hat. Der Komplex setzt sich aus einem langen niedrigen Baukörper längs der Bernstorffgade und dem sich darüber erhebenden Turm mit den Hotelzimmern zusammen. Die konstruktive Ausbildung des Hochhauses ist nicht ganz so klar, wie es beim ersten Eindruck scheinen mag. Die tragenden Stützen stehen zwar innen, und die Außenwände haben keine tragende Funktion, aber die Curtain Walls verdecken in jeder Etage hohe Betonbrüstungen, die von den feuerpolizeilichen Bestimmungen vorgeschrieben wurden. Die dänischen Brandschutzbehörden sind nicht ganz so liberal wie ihre amerikanischen Kollegen, wenn es sich um Hotelbauten von großer Höhe handelt.

Die Innengestaltung zeigt überall die sorgfältige Detailarbeit Jacobsens, besonders die Treppe zwischen der Eingangshalle und dem Vestibül im ersten Stock und der originelle Wintergarten, der durch zwei Geschosse reicht. Auch die kurzen intimen Hotelflure sind gemütlich und freundlich gestaltet. An manchen anderen Stellen werden allerdings auch Kompromisse zwischen dem Architekten und der konventionelleren Einstellung der Hotelleitung spürbar, so bei der Möblierung der Hotelzimmer und des Restaurants. Dennoch muß die einheitliche Gestaltung bewundert werden, die Jacobsen hat durchführen können, von der Außenreklame bis zu den Möbeln und den Salzstreuern und Aschenbechern auf den Eßtischen.

Der Bau liegt nicht weit vom Rathaus und dem alten Teil von Kopenhagen entfernt, und seine große Höhe und dominierende Lage gab Anlaß zu vielen Diskussionen. Aber es besteht kein Zweifel, daß er mit seiner architektonischen Qualität und seiner einfachen prismatischen Form ein wertvolles, verbindendes Element für einen Stadtteil geworden ist, dem es in jeder Weise an Charakter mangelte. Die ständig wechselnde Spiegelung von Himmel und Wolken in den großen Glasflächen betont noch die Eleganz des Baues und gibt ihm einen besonderen Akzent.

Auf dem Gebiete des Verwaltungs- und Bürobaus erwartet Arne Jacobsen eine neue große Aufgabe mit dem Neubau der dänischen Nationalbank an der Holmen Kirche in Kopenhagen (Seite 137). Im Herbst 1961 erhielt er hier den ersten Preis bei einem engeren Wettbewerb für ein Projekt, das sich durch eine souveräne, klare und einfache Gliederung der Gesamtanlage auszeichnet. Der fünfgeschossige Hauptflügel erstreckt sich bis zum Hafen hinunter, und

attitude. Admittedly, the client should not bow to the moods of the architect; but he should, once his programme is formulated, let the architect enjoy a certain amount of liberty within this framework. Seeing how consistently Arne Jacobsen has been able to realise so many of his projects, one might be tempted to assume that Jacobsen was a kind of architectural dictator. But this is not the case; he has always tried to understand and to realise the wishes of his clients, to distinguish between essential and non-essential features, and to solve his tasks with this aim in view. During the further developments of the project, he merely insists that the architect's work should be respected — a demand which, in view of his great expert knowledge, is thoroughly justified.

Up to now, his latest major work in the sphere of what has become known as "international constructivism" is the SAS ("Scandinavian Airlines System") building in Copenhagen (page 120). With this building, too, it is apparent that Arne Jacobsen derived inspiration from the United States. The complex consists of a long, low block facing Bernstorffsgade, overtowered by the multi-storey block of the hotel. The structural design of the tower block is not quite as simple as it may appear at first glance. True, the bearing stanchions are inside, and the outer walls have no bearing functions; but at each floor, the curtain walls cover high concrete parapets which had been insisted upon as a fire precaution. The Danish fire protection authorities are not quite as liberal as their American counterparts when dealing with multi-storey hotels.

The entire interior design bears witness to the careful detailed attention paid to it by Jacobsen; this applies in particular, to the stairs which connect the vestibule with the first floor foyer, and to the original conservatory which extends through two storeys. The short and intimate hotel corridors create a congenial and friendly atmosphere. There are, admittedly, at some other places, signs of a compromise between the architect and the more conventional attitude of his client, e.g. in the furnishing of the hotel rooms and of the restaurant. Even so, one cannot but admire the integral design which Jacobsen has been enabled to bring about, ranging from the outdoor advertisements to the furniture and to the condiment sets and ashtrays on the dining tables.

The building occupies a site not far from Copenhagen's Town Hall and old city, and its great height and dominating position gave rise to many discussions. There is however no doubt that, with its architectural quality and its simple prismatic shape, the building has become a valuable and integrating element in a part of the town which had lacked character in every respect. The ever changing reflections of sky and clouds in the large glass frontages emphasize and accentuate the elegance of the building. In the sphere of office and administration buildings, Arne Jacobsen is now confronted with another great task for the new building of the Danish National Bank at Holmenskirke, Copenhagen (page 137). In the autumn of 1961, he was awarded the First Prize in a limited competition for a project which is distinguished by a supremely convincing and simple arrangement. The five-storey main block extends down to the harbour, its pure cubic shape being inspired by the large old warehouses in the vicinity which were erected towards the end of the 18th century during Copenhagen's great trading era.

Arne Jacobsen's ability of finding artistically mature solutions for purely functional tasks has stood in particularly good stead with a number of industrial buildings. Major and minor buildings are designed with a brilliantly sure touch; they are concentrated in but a few simple units which are then organically fused into an architectural entity. Both with Carl Christensen's factory at Ålborg, 1957 (page 112) and with Tom's Factory, 1961 (page 138), the dominating

seine rein kubische Form ist von den in der Nähe liegenden großen alten Speichern inspiriert, die gegen Ende des 18. Jahrhunderts während der großen Handelszeit Kopenhagens errichtet wurden.

Arne Jacobsens Fähigkeit, für rein funktionelle Aufgaben künstlerisch abgeklärte Lösungen zu finden, ist besonders einer Reihe von Industriebauten zugute gekommen. Größere und kleinere Anlagen sind mit souveräner Sicherheit entworfen und auf wenige einfache Baukörper konzentriert, die dann organisch zu einer architektonischen Einheit zusammengefaßt sind. Sowohl bei der Fabrik von Carl Christensen von 1957 in Ålborg (Seite 112) als auch bei der Schokoladenfabrik Tom, 1961 (Seite 138) ist die dominierende Wirkung großer Schornsteine im Kontrast zu ausgedehnten Fabrikhallen und kleineren Bürobauten für das Gesamtbild der Anlage sehr wirkungsvoll ausgenutzt. Diese Fabrik zeigt auch, daß Jacobsen das Bauen mit vorgefertigten Betonelementen genau so sicher beherrscht wie die Detaillierung aufwendiger Inneneinrichtungen. Das Ausstellungs- und Werkstattgebäude von Massey-Harris (Seite 110) wurde 1953 bei der Internationalen Architekturausstellung der zweiten Biennale von São Paulo mit einem Ehrenpreis ausgezeichnet. Von der ganzen Hauptfassade des Gebäudes mit ihren großen Ausstellungsfenstern geht eine beträchtliche Werbewirkung für die Firma aus. Leider ist der Bau in den letzten Jahren durch eine dominierende Reklame auf dem Dach verunstaltet worden, für die Jacobsen nicht verantwortlich gemacht werden kann.

Eine Anzahl Einfamilienhäuser der späteren Jahre zeigen deutlich Jacobsens Fähigkeit, eine innige Beziehung zwischen seiner Architektur und der dänischen Landschaft herzustellen. Er hat sowohl einfache, als auch besonders große und exklusive Häuser gebaut, die alle sehr individuell gestaltet sind und die Geländeverhältnisse, die Aussicht und vorhandene Bepflanzung des jeweiligen Grundstücks berücksichtigen. Starke Geländeneigungen bestimmten weitgehend die Gestaltung der Häuser in Holte von 1954 (Seite 6), in Kalundborg von 1956 und am Prinsessestien in Lyngby von 1959 (Seite 18), wo ein hochliegendes Wohngeschoß mit guter Aussicht über ein geschlossenes Untergeschoß mit Nebenräumen auskragt. Beim Haus am Mosehøjvej in Ordrup (1960, Seite 22) boten sich Aussichtsmöglichkeiten in beiden Richtungen quer zum Geländeabfall, die zu der Konzeption des auskragenden Obergeschosses führten. Sehr schön ist auch die Lage zweier großer Grundstücke am Øresund für die großen Einfamilienhäuser C. A. Møller von 1951 (Seite 4) und Ruthwen Jürgensen von 1956 (Seite 8) ausgenutzt. In beiden Fällen waren sowohl der Wunsch nach bestmöglicher Aussicht gegen Osten über den Sund als auch die Forderung nach Besonnung am Nachmittag gleichzeitig zu erfüllen, und diese Schwierigkeit hat zu besonders interessanten Grundrißlösungen geführt. Das Innere des Hauses Ruthwen Jürgensen läßt durch die Verbindung der verschiedenen Teile des Wohnflügels zwanglose Raumfolgen entstehen, und bei der Möblierung ist die enge Zusammenarbeit zwischen Bauherrn und Architekten zu spüren.

Dagegen lag dem kreisrunden Wohnhaus für den Direktor der Odden Røgeri (1957, Seite 16) eine eher formalistische Idee zugrunde. Der Gedanke des Zukunftshauses von 1929 ist hier mit großer artistischer Eleganz verwirklicht. Die zur Fensterseite immer breiter werdenden Räume haben zwar eine sehr vorteilhafte Belichtung, sind aber recht schwierig zu möblieren. Das von Jacobsen 1961 fertiggestellte Haus für Frau Gertie Wandel in Ordrup (Seite 25) liegt versteckt hinter den Hecken einer Villenstraße und bildet den vornehmen und zugleich einfachen Rahmen für das Leben der berufstätigen Hausherrin.

In den späteren Jahren hat sich Arne Jacobsen auch für Projekte im Ausland interessiert. 1956 erhielt er den ersten Preis in einem

effect of high chimneys contrasting with extensive factory halls and minor office buildings has been most effectively brought to bear on the overall picture of the group. The buildings of Toms Fabrikker also bear witness to the fact that Jacobsen's touch is equally sure with series-produced concrete units as it is with the detailed design of more expensive interiors. The exhibition and workshop buildings of Messrs. Massey-Harris (page 110) obtained a Citation at the International Architectural Exhibition of the Second Biennale at Sao Paulo in 1953. The entire main frontage of the building with its large display windows provides a considerable publicity value to the firm. Unfortunately, the building has been spoiled recently by a huge roof advertisement for which Jacobsen cannot be held responsible.

A number of detached houses built in recent years clearly demonstrate Jacobsen's ability of creating an intimate relationship between his architecture and the Danish landscape. He has built simple as well as large and exclusive houses; all of them are of highly individual design in which the topographical conditions, the view and the existing vegetation of the site are taken into account. Steeply sloping ground governed the design of his houses at Holte in 1954 (page 6), Kalundborg in 1956 and at Prinsessestien, Lyngby, in 1959 (page 18) where a high-level living room floor affording a good view projects over an enclosed lower storey which contains the ancillary rooms. In the case of the house at Mosehøjvej in Ordrup 1960, page 22), the possibility of a view in either direction perpendicular to the sloping ground gave rise to the conception of a cantilevered upper storey. Very good use was also made of the privileged position of two large building sites at the Øresund coast for C. A. Møller's house 1951 (page 24) and Ruthwen Jürgensen's house, 1956 (page 8). In both cases, it was desired to provide the best possible view eastwards across the Sound and, at the same time, to make the most of the afternoon sun, and these requirements gave rise to particularly interesting plan solutions. In the case of Ruthwen Jürgensen's house, the arrangement of the living room wing resulted in a series of internally linked interiors, and the furniture bears witness to a close cooperation between architect and client.

In contrast, the design for the circular house built for the Director of the Herring Smoking Plant at Odden (1957, page 16) was based on a rather formalistic concept. The idea originally, in 1929, embodied in the "House of the Future" was here resumed with great artistic elegance. The rooms, widening out towards the windows, are very well designed as far as daylight is concerned; but they are difficult to furnish. Mrs. Gertie Wandel's house at Ordrup (page 25), which Jacobsen completed in 1961, lies hidden behind the hedges of a quiet residential road and forms a fine yet simple background for the life of a career woman.

In recent years, Arne Jacobsen has also taken an interest in projects abroad. In 1956, he was awarded the First Prize in a competition for a new Town Hall and Sports Hall in the town of Landskrona in Southern Sweden (pages 83 and 84). Both these designs, however, have meanwhile been completely revised and should materialize within the next few years. In 1957, Jacobsen and Kay Fisker were asked to take part in the Building Exhibition in the Hansa District of Berlin. Jacobsen's contribution consisted in four atrium houses which are, in their design and details, characteristic of his architecture. Subsequently, Jacobsen was invited to take part in several international competitions without, however, being awarded a First Prize. His project for the Town Hall at Marl in 1957 (page 107) as well as his proposal for the building of the World Health Organisation in Geneva (page 136) are distinguished by supreme solutions. His design for the Town Hall at Cologne (1958, page 106) solves

Wettbewerb für ein neues Rathaus und eine Sporthalle in der südschwedischen Stadt Landskrona (Seite 83 und 84). Jedoch sind die Entwürfe sowohl des Rathauses als auch der Halle vollständig umgearbeitet worden und sollen nun im Laufe der nächsten Jahre zur Ausführung kommen. 1957 wurden Arne Jacobsen und Kay Fisker aufgefordert, an der Bauausstellung im Berliner Hansa-Viertel teilzunehmen. Jacobsens Beitrag waren vier Atriumhäuser, die in der Ausstattung und Detaillierung charakteristisch für seine Architektur sind. Danach wurde Jacobsen zu mehreren internationalen Wettbewerben eingeladen, ohne jedoch einen ersten Preis zu erringen. Sowohl sein Projekt für das Rathaus in Marl im Jahre 1957 (Seite 107) als auch sein Vorschlag für die World's Health Organisation in Genf (Seite 136) zeichnen sich durch überlegene Lösungen aus. Sein Entwurf für das Rathaus in Köln (1958, Seite 106) stellt die schwierige Beziehung zu den alten gotischen Gebäuden durch einen vertikal gegliederten Baukörper her, der den Dimensionen der alten Bebauung angepaßt ist.

Unter den neuesten Arbeiten ist der Entwurf für das Parlamentsgebäude in Islamabad (Pakistan) besonders gelungen; er zeichnet sich durch die Einfachheit der Komposition aus, die sich auf den Gegensatz zwischen dem niedrigen Rechteck und dem beherrschenden Zylinder des Versammlungssaales beschränkt. Das Projekt beweist, wie sehr sich Arne Jacobsen durch die großen internationalen Aufgabenstellungen anregen ließ, seine Fähigkeiten zu erweitern. Heute meistert er die großen Leitgedanken ebenso gut wie das kleinste Detail, und dabei entwickelt er sich ständig weiter.

1960 erhielt Arne Jacobsen den Auftrag, ein Projekt für das St. Catherine's College in Oxford auszuführen (Seite 76), in einer Umwelt, die sowohl geistig als auch architektonisch von alter englischer Tradition beherrscht ist. Die Wahl eines Architekten aus dem Ausland für eine derartige Aufgabe mußte natürlich eine heftige Reaktion hervorrufen. Jacobsen ist mit großem Ernst an diese Arbeit herangegangen. Er wollte nicht die Formensprache der Gotik nachahmen, sondern hat eine sehr einfache Gestaltung gesucht, die der Anlage Selbständigkeit geben sollte, ohne aufdringlich zu wirken. Geschickt angeordnete perforierte Schutzblenden lassen zwar neue Anregungen aus den USA ahnen, jedoch sind diese Abschirmungen hier durchaus berechtigt und auch formal geglückt.

Arne Jacobsens Interesse erstreckt sich nicht nur auf alle Gebiete seines Fachs. Er gestaltet am liebsten selbst alle Gartenanlagen, Einrichtungen, Beleuchtungskörper und so weiter für seine eigenen Bauten und entwirft auch Standardtypen für fast alle Zweige der Kunstindustrie.

Seine Möbelentwürfe sind unorthodox, und die Möglichkeiten neuer Materialien reizen ihn besonders. Großen Erfolg hat er mit seinen dreibeinigen Stapelstühlen gehabt, bei denen Sitz und Rücken aus nur einem Stück furnierten Sperrholzes bestehen (Seite 163). Diese preiswerten Stühle fanden große Verbreitung und wurden später noch durch veränderte und verbesserte Typen mit Armlehnen und vier Beinen ergänzt (Seite 167-169). Auch viele gute Beleuchtungskörper in den Katalogen der Fabriken stammen von Arne Jacobsen (Seite 154-157). In der Silberschmiedekunst betätigte er sich ebenfalls und entwarf ein Besteck (Seite 148), das jedoch Schwierigkeiten hat, mit den vorzüglichen traditionellen Bestecken zu konkurrieren. Jacobsens Vielseitigkeit ist selten in einer Welt, in der die Spezialisierung immer mehr um sich greift und wohl auch vernünftig und notwendig ist. Aber Jacobsen will kein Spezialist sein. Er erhält durch die ständig wechselnden Aufgaben neue künstlerische Impulse und bewahrt sich seine umfassende schöpferische Kraft.

Arne Jacobsens Qualitäten liegen nicht in einer besonderen Originalität oder einer großen Phantasiefülle seiner ausgeführten Arbeiten.

the difficult problem of the relationship with the old Gothic buildings in the vicinity by means of a vertically orientated block which is adapted to the dimensions of the old buildings.

Among Jacobsen's latest works, his project for the Parliament Building at Islamabad, Pakistan, is particularly attractive; it is distinguished by the simplicity of its composition which is confined to the combination of a low rectangular block with the dominating cylinder of the Parliament Chamber. The project shows to what extent Arne Jacobsen has been able to derive inspiration for expanding his talents as a result of the great international design competitions. By now, his mastery ranges over the great guiding principles as well as the most minute details; yet he still continues to develop.

In 1960, Arne Jacobsen was commissioned to prepare a design for St. Catherine's College, Oxford (page 76), in an environment spiritually as well as architecturally governed by old English tradition. The choice of a foreign architect for such a task was bound to give rise to violent reactions. Jacobsen approached this task with great serentiy. He did not want to imitate the formal language of the Gothic but looked for a very simple design which would make the group of buildings independent in style without, however, being obtrusive. Skilfully arranged perforated shutters seem to suggest new inspirations from the United States; but they are, in the circumstances, fully justified, and are also formally successful.

Arne Jacobsen's interests are not confined to all the aspects of his own profession. He much prefers to create his own designs for the gardens, interior furnishings, light fittings, etc. of his houses and has also produced standard designs for nearly all branches of arts and crafts. His furniture designs are unorthodox, and he is particularly interested in the potentialities of new materials. He has been very successful with his three-legged stacking chairs where seat and back consist of a single piece of veneered plywood (page 163). These inexpensive chairs became very popular, and were later supplemented by modified and improved types with armrest and four legs (pages 167-169). Arne Jacobsen was also responsible for the design of many good light fittings which now feature in factory catalogues (pages 154-157). He even took an interest in silverware and designed a set of cutlery (page 148) which has, however, met with some difficulties in competing with the excellent traditional types of cutlery. Jacobsen's versatility is a rare phenomenon in a world where specialisation is increasingly predominant and, at the same time, reasonable and necessary. But Jacobsen refuses to be a specialist. From his ever-changing tasks, he continues to derive new artistic impulses, thus keeping his vast creative power alive.

Arne Jacobsen's qualities do not lie in the application, to his well-designed works, of any special originality or any unusual wealth of imagination. But he is a highly gifted architect who has a supremely sure touch in working out his designs, who is extremely neat and clear in his architecture and who, in his simplified compositions, is always aiming at a harmonic overall solution.

As a person, Arne Jacobsen is reserved. He is keenly intelligent, has a sense of humour and plenty of commonsense, and feels most comfortable within a small circle of good friends. He prefers to spend his time at the drawing board or among the eight or ten colleagues who normally work in his office. Despite the magnitude of the tasks and the careful elaboration of his projects, his office has never been enlarged any further — nor does he want it to be enlarged. Jacobsen intends to maintain direct contact with his collaborators and insists on a detailed knowledge of any drawing that leaves his office. In 1956, he was appointed Professor at the Copenhagen Academy of Arts, being honoured with a personal Professor-

Aber er ist ein hochbegabter Architekt, der seine Entwürfe mit souveräner Sicherheit ausarbeitet, in seiner Architektur außerordentlich sauber und klar ist und in seinen vereinfachten Kompositionen immer eine harmonische Gestaltung zu erreichen sucht.

Persönlich ist Arne Jacobsen zurückhaltend. Er ist klug, hat Humor und common sense und fühlt sich am wohlsten in dem kleinen Kreis guter Freunde. Er verbringt seine Zeit am liebsten am Zeichenbrett oder zwischen den acht bis zehn Mitarbeitern, die normalerweise in seinem Büro tätig sind. Trotz der Größe der Bauaufgaben und der sorgfältigen Durcharbeitung seiner Projekte hat das Büro nie einen größeren Umfang angenommen, und es soll nach seinem Wunsch auch nicht erweitert werden. Jacobsen will den direkten Kontakt mit seinen Mitarbeitern bewahren und jede Zeichnung, die sein Büro verläßt, genau kennen. 1956 wurde er als Professor an die Kunstakademie in Kopenhagen berufen. Einige Jahre lang war er auch Mitglied des Akademierats.

Mit seinen sechzig Jahren steht Arne Jacobsen mitten in der Arbeit. Er hat früh angefangen und kann deshalb schon auf eine große und reiche Tätigkeit zurückblicken. Als jungem talentiertem Mann von unbeschwerter Natur fiel ihm das Zeichnen und Entwerfen leicht. Er hatte schnell Erfolg, ohne sich viel um die technischen und geistigen Zusammenhänge zu kümmern; aber im Laufe der Jahre ist er zu einem ernsthaft arbeitenden Künstler gereift, der heute Achtung und Anerkennung von allen Seiten genießt.

Es gibt wenige dänische Architekten, die über die Grenzen des Landes hinaus bekannt geworden sind, obwohl Dänemark in seiner Architekturgeschichte Persönlichkeiten besitzt, die es ebenso wie Arne Jacobsen verdient haben würden. Aber erst in unseren Tagen ermöglicht die weltweite Aufgeschlossenheit die Bekanntschaft mit bedeutenden Künstlern auch eines kleinen Landes. Den Respekt, den Arne Jacobsen unbestreitbar und wohlverdient draußen in der Welt genießt, verdankt er in erster Linie der klaren, einfachen Gestaltung und dem hohen Niveau seiner Arbeiten. Er kann aber auch als Exponent für den Rang der Architektur in seinem eigenen Land angesehen werden wie auch für die Sorgfalt, mit der die Architekten die noch vorhandene handwerkliche Tradition pflegen. Diese Tradition muß natürlich durch die neuen technischen Möglichkeiten, Materialien und industriellen Herstellungsverfahren ergänzt werden, bleibt aber hoffentlich noch viele Jahre erhalten um der Qualität in der künftigen Architektur willen.

ship. For a number of years, he also was a Member of the Council of the Academy.

At 60 years of age, Arne Jacobsen now stands at the zenith of his work. Having made an early start, he is already able to look back on vast and rich activities. As a gifted young man of carefree nature, drawing and designing came to him easily. He gained his success rapidly without, at the time, giving much thought to the technical and spiritual associations; over the years, however, he has matured into an earnest artist who has gained universal respect and recognition.

There are but few Danish architects who have become known outside the confines of their country, and this despite the fact that, in her architectural history, Denmark has produced personalities who might have been equally deserving of such fame. But it is only in our days of world-wide intelligence that, even in a small country, leading artists have a chance of earning a wider reputation. The undoubted and well deserved respect which Arne Jacobsen enjoys throughout the world is mainly due to his lucid and simple design and to the high standard of his work. But he also stands for the high position of architecture in his own country, and for the care with which architects endeavour to cultivate the tradition of craftsmanship still in existence. This tradition must obviously be invigorated by the use of new technical potentialities, materials and industrial production methods. For the sake of future architectural standards, however, this tradition will, it may be hoped, be kept alive for many years to come.

Eigenes Sommerhaus, Gudmindrup Lyng, West-Seeland, 1937

Arne Jacobsen baute sein eigenes Sommerhaus, einen weiß gekalkten Backsteinbau, in einer Heide- und Dünenlandschaft. Der Wohnraum liegt auf einer Düne, von der aus sich ein Blick über das Kattegat bietet. Eine hölzerne Außenrampe führt von hier aus ins Freie. Der Trakt mit den Schlafräumen liegt tiefer, im Windschatten der Düne, und ist mit dem Wohnraum durch eine Treppe verbunden.

Jacobsen's Summer House, Gudmindrup Lyng, West-Zealand, 1937

Arne Jacobsen built his own summer house, a white-washed brick building, in a landscape characterised by heath and dunes. The lounge is situated on a sand hill which offers a view over the Kattegat. From here, a wooden outdoor ramp leads down to the ground. The bedroom wing lies at a lower level, in the shelter of the dune, and is connected with the lounge by a flight of stairs.

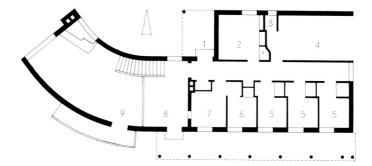

1 Grundriß M 1:250 / Plan, scale 1:250.
  1 Eingang / Entrance
  2 Gastzimmer / Guest room
  3 WC
  4 Garage
  5 Schlafzimmer / Bedroom
  6 Mädchenzimmer / Maid's room
  7 Küche / Kitchen
  8 Eßplatz / Dining area
  9 Wohnraum / Lounge
2 Treppe zwischen dem Wohnraum und dem Eßplatz, der mit den Schlafräumen in gleicher Höhe liegt.
  Stairs connecting the lounge with the dining area which is at the same level as the bedrooms.

3 Ansicht von Osten. Der Dachüberhang ruht
  auf Stützen und wirkt als Pergola.
  View from the East. The projecting roof is
  supported by stanchions and gives the impression of a pergola.
4 Ansicht von Westen.
  View from the West.

Haus C. A. Møller, Vedbæk, 1951

Das Grundstück fällt zum Øresund hin ab. Das Wohnhaus hat Aussicht sowohl nach Osten auf den Sund wie — von der geschützten Terrasse aus — nach Westen. In einem gesondert liegenden Baukörper ist außer der Garage eine Gärtnerwohnung untergebracht, deren Obergeschoß mit den Schlafzimmern über die Verbindungsmauer zwischen den beiden Häusern auskragt. Durch diese Anordnung entstand ein intimer Gartenhof zwischen den beiden Bauten. Die Außenwände bestehen teils aus weiß gekalktem Backsteinmauerwerk, teils aus holzverkleidetem Fachwerk.

C. A. Møller's House, Vedbæk, 1951

The ground slopes down to the Øresund. The house enjoys a view eastwards towards the Sound as well as, from the protected terrace, towards the West. A separate building accommodates the garage and a dwelling for the gardener; its top floor containing the bedrooms projects over the wall connecting the two buildings. With this arrangement, a private patio has been created between the two buildings. The outer walls are partly of white-washed brick, partly of half-timbering with wood board cladding.

1 Ansicht von Süden mit der Gärtnerwohnung links und dem Wohnhaus rechts.
View from the South, with the gardener's dwelling on the left, and the main building on the right.

2 Ansicht von Westen entlang der Verbindungsmauer.
View from the West, along the connecting
wall.
3 Ansicht von Osten (vom Øresund).
View from the East, i. e. from the Øresund.
4 Ansicht von Westen (Eingangsseite) mit
der Gärtnerwohnung im Vordergrund.
View from the West, i. e. from the entrance
side, with the gardener's dwelling in the
foreground.

5 Grundriß 1:250.
Plan, scale 1:250.
  1 Eingang / Entrance
  2 Wohnraum / Lounge
  3 Eßzimmer / Dining room
  4 Küche / Kitchen
  5 Gastzimmer / Guest room
  6 Schlafzimmer / Bedroom
  7 WC
  8 Bad / Bath
  9 Ankleideraum / Dressing room
  10 Wohnung des Gärtners / Gardener's
     dwelling
  11 Waschküche / Laundry
  12 Garage
  13 Fahrräder / Bicycles

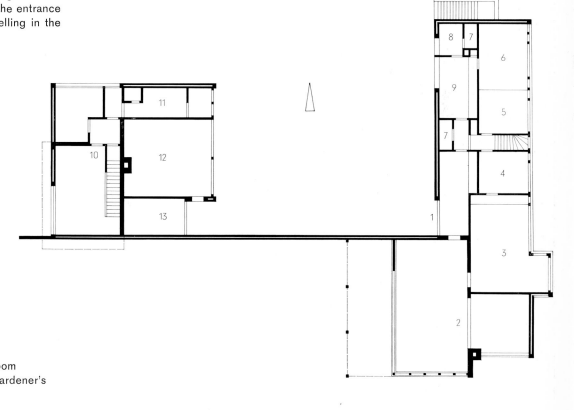

Haus Henning Simony, Geelsvej, Holte, 1954

Bei dem Grundstück handelt es sich um eine ehemalige Kiesgrube. Die beträchtlichen Niveauunterschiede des Geländes waren für die Gestaltung des Hauses entscheidend. Der Eingang an der Nordseite führt in das mittlere Geschoß mit Eßplatz und Küche. Wohn- und Schlafraum liegen eine halbe Etage tiefer in der Höhe des Gartens. Das oberste Stockwerk, das über die Stützmauer am Rande der Kiesgrube auskragt, nimmt die Kinderzimmer auf.

Henning Simony's House, Geelsvej, Holte, 1954

The building stands on the site of an old gravel pit. The considerable differences in level had a decisive influence on the design of the house. The North entrance leads to the intermediate level with dining area and kitchen. Lounge and bedroom are half-a-storey lower at garden level. The top floor, which projects over the retaining wall at the edge of the gravel pit, contains the nurseries.

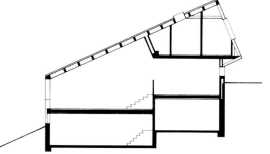

1 Blick vom Eßplatz zum Wohnraum.
   View from dining area towards the lounge.

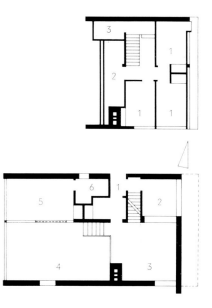

2 Schnitt von Westen nach Osten M 1:250.
   Section, West to East, scale 1:250.
3 Grundriß oberstes Geschoß M 1:250.
   Top floor plan, scale 1:250.
   1 Schlafzimmer / Bedrooms
   2 Abstellraum / Spare room
   3 WC
4 Grundriß Hauptgeschoß M 1:250.
   Main floor plan, scale 1:250.
   1 Eingang / Entrance
   2 Küche / Kitchen
   3 Eßplatz / Dining area
   4 Wohnraum / Lounge
   5 Schlafzimmer / Bedroom
   6 Bad und WC / Bathroom and W. C.

6

5 Kinderzimmer.
  Nursery.

6 Ansicht von Südosten.
  View from South-East.
7 Ansicht von Südwesten.
  View from South-West.

Haus Ruthwen Jürgensen, Vedbæk, 1956

Der Grundriß des Hauses, einer dreiflügeligen Anlage, ist bestimmt durch die Aussicht nach Osten auf den Øresund und durch die günstigste Ausnutzung des Sonnenstandes. Der Hauptflügel wurde als Stahlrahmenkonstruktion errichtet und innen wie außen mit Holzriemen verkleidet. Die beiden anderen Trakte sind Backsteinbauten mit großen Holzfenstern nach Süden. Die Einrichtung des Hauses entstand in enger Zusammenarbeit zwischen Bauherrn und Architekten; ein großer Teil der Möbel wurde von Arne Jacobsen selbst entworfen. Auch die Bepflanzung von Garten, Hof und Wintergarten wurde nach Plänen Jacobsens ausgeführt.

Ruthwen Jürgensen's House, Vedbæk, 1956

The plan of the three-winged house is governed by the eastward view across the Sound and by the desire to make the most of the sunlight. The main part of the building is a steel frame structure with internal as well as external boarding. The other two wings are brick buildings with large wooden-frame windows facing South. The furnishing was designed in close collaboration between owner and architect; much of the furniture was designed by Arne Jacobsen himself. Even the flora of garden, courtyard and conservatory was arranged in accordance with Jacobsen's designs.

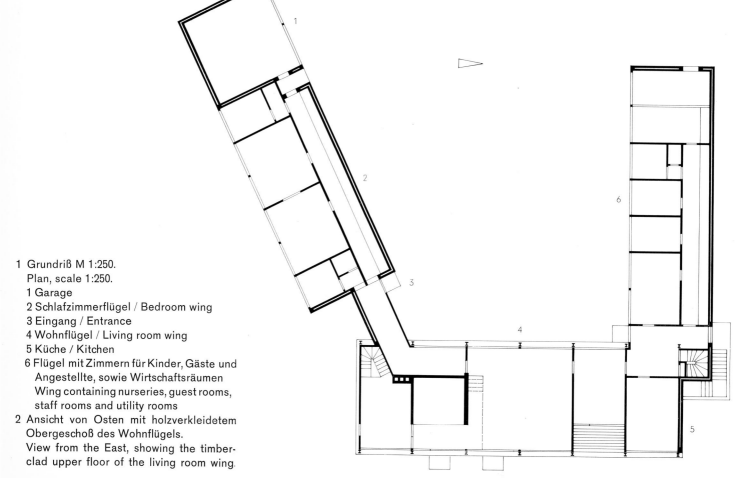

1 Grundriß M 1:250.
  Plan, scale 1:250.
  1 Garage
  2 Schlafzimmerflügel / Bedroom wing
  3 Eingang / Entrance
  4 Wohnflügel / Living room wing
  5 Küche / Kitchen
  6 Flügel mit Zimmern für Kinder, Gäste und
    Angestellte, sowie Wirtschaftsräumen
    Wing containing nurseries, guest rooms,
    staff rooms and utility rooms
2 Ansicht von Osten mit holzverkleidetem
  Obergeschoß des Wohnflügels.
  View from the East, showing the timber-
  clad upper floor of the living room wing.

8

3 Der windgeschützte Hof öffnet sich nach
Westen. Die Fenster des Flügels mit Zimmern für Gäste, Kinder und Angestellte
sind nach Süden orientiert.
The wind-protected courtyard opens west-
wards. The windows of the wing containing
the guest rooms, nurseries and staff rooms
face South.

4 Terrasse vor dem nach Südosten abge-
schwenkten Schlafzimmerflügel. Im Hintergrund die Stirnseite des Wohnflügels mit
den Fenstern des Wintergartens und dem
Balkon des Herrenzimmers im Obergeschoß.
Terrace in front of the bedroom wing
which is turned towards South-East. In the
background, the end of the living room
wing with the conservatory windows and
the smoking room balcony on the upper
floor.
5 Außentreppe von der Terrasse im Osten
zum Herrenzimmer.
Outdoor stairs from the East Terrace to
the smoking room.

6 Blick vom Eßzimmer in den Wohnraum
mit innenliegender Treppe zum Herrenzimmer im Obergeschoß. Die Unterteilung
der doppelseitig belichteten Raumfolge
ist nicht bis zur schräg ansteigenden Decke
hochgeführt und beeinträchtigt daher nicht
den großzügigen Raumeindruck.
View from the dining room into the lounge,
with the indoor stairway leading to the
upper floor smoking room. The partitions
of these rooms which receive daylight from
both sides, are not extended to the inclined ceiling so that they do not impair the
impression of a spacious and generously
lighted room.

7 Das Orchideenfenster des Wintergartens
geht nach Osten und gibt die Aussicht
über den Øresund frei. Die Außentreppe
führt von der Ostterrasse zum Herrenzimmer im Obergeschoß.
The orchid window of the conservatory
faces East, permitting a view over the
Sound. The outdoor stairs lead from the
East Terrace to the upper floor smoking
room.

Sommerhaus Kokfelt, Tisvilde, 1957

Alle Räume des Hauses sind nach Westen orientiert. Um dem Wohnraum eine zusätzliche Aussicht nach Norden über das Kattegat zu geben, wurde der Baukörper auf ein schmales Untergeschoß gestellt, in dem die Garage und ein Abstellraum untergebracht sind. Die Ständerkonstruktion des Hauses ist außen und innen mit Brettern verkleidet.

Kokfelt's Summer House, Tisvilde, 1957

All the rooms in the house face West. To give the lounge the benefit of an additional view towards the Kattegat in the North, the main body of the cottage was placed on a narrow lower storey which contains a garage and a shed. The house has a stanchion framework with external and internal boarding.

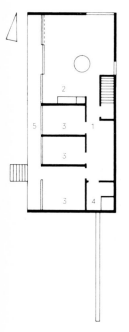
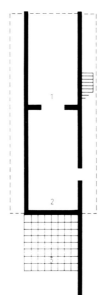

1 Grundriß Obergeschoß M 1:250.
  Upper floor plan, scale 1:250.
  1 Flur / Corridor
  2 Wohnraum mit Kochnische / Lounge
    with kitchenette
  3 Schlafzimmer / Bedrooms
  4 Bad und WC / Bath and W. C.
  5 Balkon / Balcony
2 Grundriß Untergeschoß M 1:250.
  Lower floor plan, scale 1:250.
  1 Garage
  2 Abstellraum / Shed
  3 Terrasse / Terrace
3 Blick in den Wohnraum mit dem Aussichtsfenster nach Norden.
  View of the lounge with the picture window
  facing North.

14

4 Ansicht von Südwesten mit Treppe von
 der Terrasse zum Garten.
 View from South-West with stairs leading
 from the terrace to the garden.
5 Ansicht von Norden.
 View from the North.

Haus Sjællands Odde, Odden Havn, 1957

Dieses Einfamilienhaus wurde für den Direktor der A/S Sjællands Oddes Fiskerøgeri gebaut, einer Heringsräucherei, deren Gebäude Arne Jacobsen 1943 errichtet hatte. Der kreisrunde Grundriß ist zum Teil bedingt durch Form und Vegetation des Grundstücks, sowie durch den Wunsch nach bestmöglichem Windschutz und weitgehender Besonnung der Räume. Der Windfang führt in die zentral gelegene Diele, von der man in die einzelnen Räume gelangt. Die Außenwand besteht aus tragenden Stahlelementen mit einem Achsmaß von 72 cm und geschlossenen Wandfeldern aus doppelten Stahltafeln.

House Sjællands Odde, Odden Havn, 1957

This house was erected for the manager of "A/S Sjællands Oddes Fiskerøgeri", a herring smoking plant built by Arne Jacobsen in 1943. The circular plan has been adopted partly because of the shape and vegetation of the site, and partly because it was desired to obtain the best possible wind protection and sunlight conditions. The porch leads to the hall in the centre which gives access to the different rooms. The outer wall consists of bearing steel units, based on a module of 72 cm (2ft. 4³/₈in.) and comprising solid wall panels with double steel sheeting.

1 Grundriß M 1:250.
  Plan, scale 1:250.
  1 Eingang / Entrance
  2 Diele / Hall
  3 Wohnraum / Lounge
  4 Eßzimmer / Dining room
  5 Küche / Kitchen
  6 Schlafzimmer / Bedrooms
  7 Bad und WC / Bath and W.C.
  8 Wirtschaftsräume / Utility rooms
2 Ansicht von Südosten mit den Kaminschloten der Heringsräucherei im Hintergrund.
  View from South-East, with the chimneys of the herring smoking plant in the background.

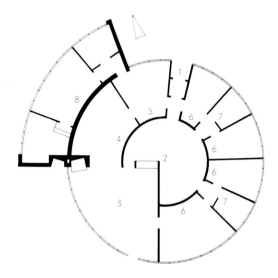

3 Der weiß gekalkte Backsteinbau der Heringsräucherei mit breiten Schornsteinen
und großem Pultdach liegt an einem zum
Kattegat hin abfallenden Hang.
The white-washed brick building of the
herring smoking plant with its wide chimneys and large pent roof lies on a slope
facing the Kattegat.

4 Blick von der Terrasse (mit Außenkamin)
in den Wohnraum.
View from the terrace (with barbecue)
into the lounge.

5 Blick vom Wohnraum ins Speisezimmer,
das von einem kreisrunden Oberlicht über
dem Eßtisch Licht empfängt. Rechts hinter
dem Regal die in der Mitte des Hauses
gelegene Diele.
View from the lounge into the dining room
which receives daylight through a circular
fanlight above the dining table. On the
right, behind the shelves, the hall which
occupies the centre of the house.

Haus Sorgenfri (Haus Erik Siesby), Prinsessestien, Lyngby, 1959

Das Haus liegt auf einem stark abfallenden Grundstück, dessen Höhenunterschied von dem gemauerten Untergeschoß aufgenommen wird. Der eigentliche Wohnteil in leichter, mit Holz verschalter Ständerkonstruktion steht auf einer ausgekragten Holzbalkenlage, die auf dem Untergeschoß aufsitzt. Alle Schlafräume sind nach Süden mit Aussicht über den Lyngby-See orientiert. Der Wohnraum öffnet sich nach Westen auf eine Terrasse, von der eine Treppe in den Garten führt. Das Untergeschoß enthält Nebenräume und eine Bibliothek, die über einen kleinen geschützten Hof von der Ostseite her belichtet ist.

House Sorgenfri (Erik Siesby's House), Prinsessestien, Lyngby, 1959

The house is situated on a steep slope, the difference in level being compensated by a brick-built lower storey. The dwelling proper, a boarded light-weight stanchion structure, stands on a projecting tier of timber beams resting on the lower storey. All the bedrooms face South, with a view across Lake Lyngby. The lounge faces West, towards a terrace connected with the garden by a flight of stairs. The lower storey contains utility rooms and a library which receives its daylight through a small, protected courtyard on the East Side.

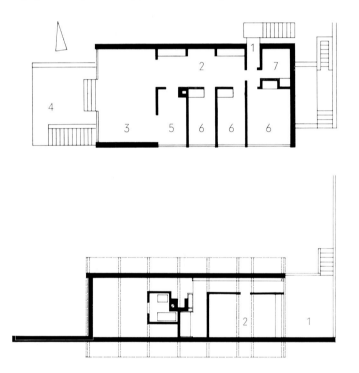

1 Grundriß Obergeschoß M 1:250.
  Upper floor plan, scale 1:250.
  1 Eingang / Entrance
  2 Diele / Hall
  3 Wohnraum / Lounge
  4 Terrasse / Terrace
  5 Küche / Kitchen
  6 Schlafzimmer / Bedrooms
  7 Bad und WC / Bathroom and W. C.
2 Grundriß Untergeschoß M 1:250.
  Lower floor plan, scale 1:250.
  1 Versenkter Hof / Sunken courtyard
  2 Bibliothek / Library
3 Ansicht von Süden.
  View from the South.

Haus Edwin Jensen, Mosehøjvej, Ordrup, 1960

Auch dieses Einfamilienhaus nutzt die Hanglage aus. Das stark nach Norden abfallende Grundstück bietet gute Aussicht nach Osten und Westen. Den Niveauunterschied gleicht ein massiv wirkendes Untergeschoß aus. Der Wohnraum springt weit über dieses Sockelgeschoß vor und ist mit einer Wandscheibe aus Holz nach Norden geschlossen; die Belichtung erfolgt im ausgekragten Teil des Baukörpers durch zwei große Fenster nach Osten und Westen. Die Schlafzimmer sind nach Osten orientiert, während Küche, Kinderzimmer und eine kleine Personalwohnung nach Westen gerichtet sind. Das Untergeschoß enthält u. a. einen großen Raum für Festlichkeiten. Das Haus ist in Backstein ausgeführt, die lange westliche Fensterwand in Stahlstützen mit Teakholzbrüstungen.

Edwin Jensen's House, Mosehøjvej, Ordrup, 1960

This house, too, makes use of a sloping ground. The marked northward declivity of the ground offers good views towards East and West. The difference in level is compensated by a massive-looking lower storey. The lounge projects dramatically above this lower storey and is protected on the North side by a wooden wall panel. The projecting part receives its daylight through two large windows, facing East and West, respectively. The bedrooms face East whilst kitchen, nursery and a small dwelling for the staff face West. The lower floor contains, inter alia, a large banqueting room. The house is brick-built; the long window frontage on the West side has steel stanchions and teak-wood spandrel panels.

3 Terrasse vor der Westseite.
West-side terrace.

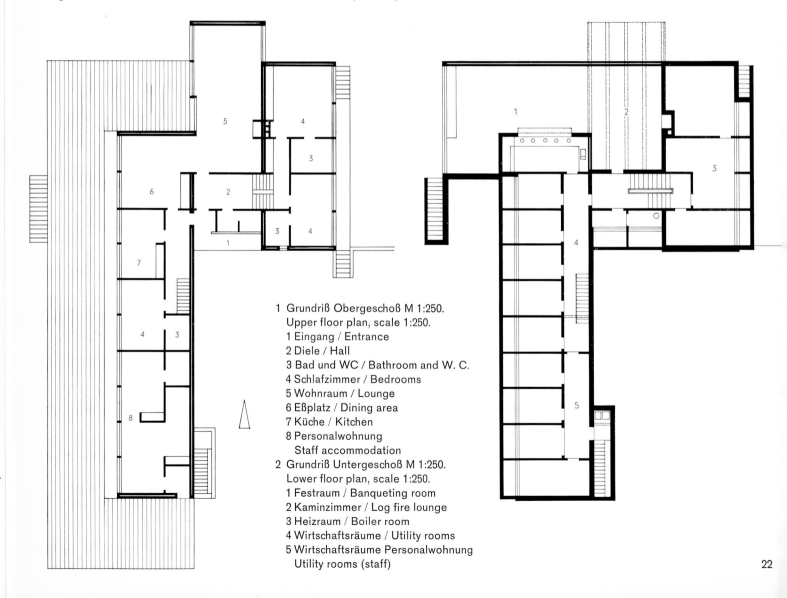

1 Grundriß Obergeschoß M 1:250.
Upper floor plan, scale 1:250.
1 Eingang / Entrance
2 Diele / Hall
3 Bad und WC / Bathroom and W. C.
4 Schlafzimmer / Bedrooms
5 Wohnraum / Lounge
6 Eßplatz / Dining area
7 Küche / Kitchen
8 Personalwohnung
  Staff accommodation
2 Grundriß Untergeschoß M 1:250.
Lower floor plan, scale 1:250.
1 Festraum / Banqueting room
2 Kaminzimmer / Log fire lounge
3 Heizraum / Boiler room
4 Wirtschaftsräume / Utility rooms
5 Wirtschaftsräume Personalwohnung
  Utility rooms (staff)

22

2 Ansicht von Osten.
  View from the East.
3 Bepflanzte Terrasse vor der nördlichen
  Fensterwand des Wohnraums.
  Garden terrace along the North side
  windows of the living room.

26

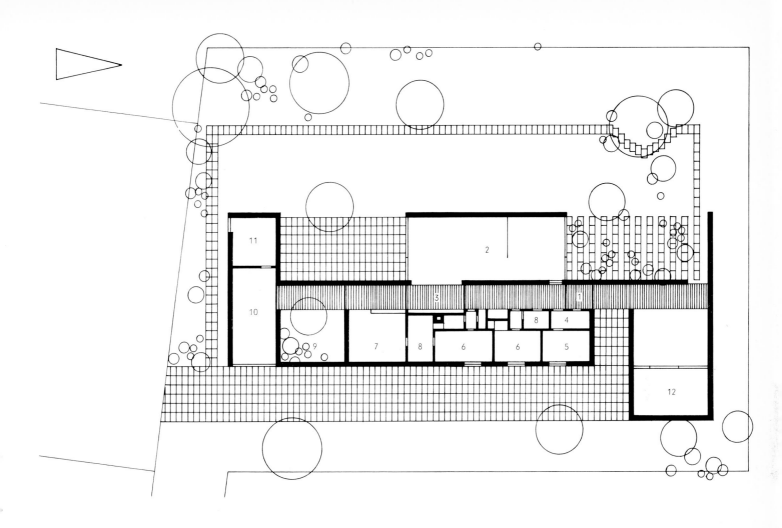

4 Grundriß M 1:250 / Plan, scale 1:250.
  1 Windfang / Porch
  2 Wohnraum mit Eßplatz / Lounge with dining area
  3 Kaminplatz / Log fire
  4 Anrichte / Pantry
  5 Küche / Kitchen
  6 Zimmer / Room
  7 Schlafzimmer / Bedrooms
  8 Bad und WC / Bathroom and W.C.
  9 Gartenhof / Patio
10 Garage
11 Heizraum / Boiler room
12 Waschküche / Laundry

5 Schlafzimmer und Blick in den langen Gang, der die Achse des Hauses bildet und der zum Teil (mit Regalwand und Kamin) in den Wohnbereich einbezogen ist.
Bedroom, and view along the long corridor which forms the centre line of the building. One part of the corridor, with bookcase wall and fireplace, forms part of the living room area.

27

3 Wohnbebauung Bellavista. Ansicht des südlichen Flügels von Südwesten. Die Fassadenflucht ist so gestaffelt, daß jede Wohnung Aussicht auf den Sund hat. Die in Backstein errichteten Bauten sind verputzt und geweißt, über den großen Fenstern liegen verdeckte Stahlträger.

Bellavista Housing Estate. View of South wing, seen from the South-West. The façades are staggered in such a way that each dwelling has the benefit of the view over the Sound. The brick buildings are plastered and white-washed. The large window openings are spanned by hidden steel beams.

4 Wohnbebauung Bellavista. Lageplan M 1:1000.

Bellavista Housing Estate. Layout plan, scale 1:1000.

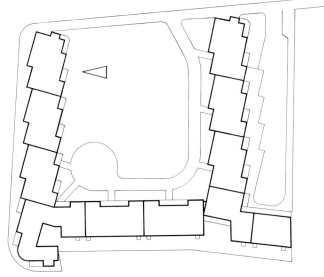

5 Wohnbebauung Bellavista. Ansicht des
südlichen Flügels von Südosten.
Bellavista Housing Estate. View of the
South wing, from the South-East.
6 Wohnbebauung Bellavista. Grundriß Normalgeschoß M 1:400 / Bellavista Housing
Estate. Typical floor plan, scale 1:400.
1 Diele / Hall
2 Küche / Kitchen
3 Bad und WC / Bathroom and W.C.
4 Schlafzimmer / Bedrooms
5 Wohnraum / Sitting room

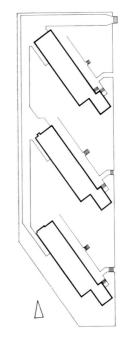

Siedlung am Hørsholmvej, Jægersborg, Gentofte, 1947

Die Siedlung wurde erbaut aus den Mitteln einer Stiftung für den Wohnungsbau der Gemeinde Gentofte, die — als Anerkennung für den Einsatz der dänischen Jugend während des Krieges — jungen Ehepaaren zugute kommen sollte. Die Anlage umfaßt drei parallele dreigeschossige Wohnblöcke mit hohen Kellergeschossen, die, gut orientiert, schräg zu der Verkehrsachse Hørsholmvej liegen. An jeden Südostgiebel schließt sich ein eingeschossiger Kopfbau an, der Kindergarten, Kinderkrippe und Heizerwohnung aufnimmt. Die Bauten sind in Backsteinmauerwerk mit Dächern aus blaugrauem Eternitschiefer ausgeführt.

Hørsholmvej Housing Estate, Jægersborg, Gentofte, 1947

The housing estate was financed by a special fund set aside by the Borough of Gentofte for the housing of young married couples, in recognition of the part played by Danish youth during the War. The estate contains three parallel three-storey blocks with high basements; the well orientated blocks lie at an angle to the main road, Hørsholmvej. At the South-East end of each block lies a single-storey annex which contains a kindergarten, crèche, and a flat for the boiler attendant. The buildings are erected in brick, with blue-grey asbestos cement slate roofs.

38

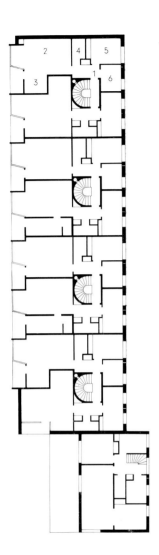

3 Grundriß Normalgeschoß M 1:400.
   Typical floor plan, scale 1:400.
   1 Eingang / Entrance
   2 Wohnzimmer / Living room
   3 Eßplatz / Dining area
   4 Bad und WC / Bathroom and W.C.
   5 Schlafzimmer / Bedroom
   6 Küche / Kitchen
4 Ansicht von Süden. Die Balkonbrüstungen
   sind aus vorgefertigten Betonelementen.
   View from the South. The balcony parapets consist of prefabricated concrete
   units.
5 Ansicht von Südosten auf die Giebel der
   dreigeschossigen Wohnblöcke und die eingeschossigen Kopfbauten.
   View from South-East, showing the end
   walls of the three-storey blocks of flats
39 with the single-storey annexes.

8 Søholm 1. Blick vom Wohnraum im Obergeschoß auf den Eßplatz.
Søholm No. 1. View from the upper floor lounge into the dining space below.

9 Søholm 1. Kamin im Hause des Architekten mit an der Wand befestigten Siegeln.
Søholm No. 1. Fireplace in the architect's own house, with seals fixed to the wall.

10 Søholm 1. Wohnraum im südöstlichsten Kettenhaus, das Jacobsen selber bewohnt.
Søholm No. 1. Lounge of the chain house at the South-East end, occupied by Jacobsen himself.

11 Søholm 1. Ansicht von Nordosten.
Søholm No. 1. View from North-East.

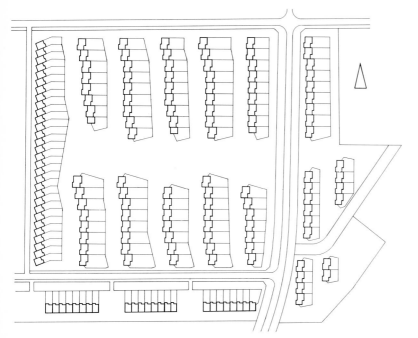

Reihenhaussiedlung Islevvænge, Rødovre, 1951

Die eingeschossigen Hauszeilen aus gelbem Ziegelstein und grauen Eternit-Dächern wurden für die gemeinnützige Wohnungsbaugesellschaft Rødovre errichtet. Die Häuser besitzen kleine Gärten und sind um eine gemeinsame Grünfläche gruppiert.

Islevvænge Housing Estate, Rødovre, 1951

The single-storey terrace houses of yellow brick with grey asbestos cement roofs were built for the non-profit making Rødovre Housing Association. The houses have small gardens and are grouped around a communal open space.

1 Ansicht von Nordwesten.
  View from North-West.
2 Lageplan M 1:3000.
  Layout plan, scale 1:3000.

1 Ansicht von Südwesten.
  View from South-West.
2 Grundriß 1. Obergeschoß M 1:500.
  First floor plan, scale 1:500.
  1 Eingang / Entrance
  2 Wohnraum mit Loggia
    Lounge with loggia
  3 Zimmer / Rooms
  4 Bad und WC / Bathroom and W. C.
  5 Küche / Kitchen

Wohnblock Alléhusene, Jægersborg Allé, Gentofte, 1952

Der Wohnblock liegt in der Nähe der Ibstrupparken-Bebauung (Seite 36). Die versetzte Anordnung der Loggien schützt vor Einblick. Durch die Ausschwenkungen der Ostfassade sind Eingänge von Norden und Besonnung der Küchen von Südosten erreicht worden. Baumaterialien waren wieder gelber Backstein und Eternit für die Dächer.

Block of Flats at Alléhusene, Jægersborg Allé, Gentofte, 1952

The block of flats is situated in the vicinity of Ibstrupparken Housing Estate (page 36). The staggered arrangement of the loggias ensures greater privacy. By varying the angles of the East façade, it has been possible to obtain entrances from the North and sunlight access for the kitchens from South-East. The building materials are again yellow brick and asbestos cement roofing.

1 Ansicht von Nordosten auf die Ostfassade
   mit den Hauseingängen.
   View, from North-East, of the East front
   with the entrances.
2 Grundriß Obergeschoß M 1:250.
   Upper floor plan, scale 1:250.
   1 Schlafzimmer / Bedrooms
   2 Bad und WC / Bathroom and W. C.
3 Grundriß Erdgeschoß M 1:250.
   Ground floor plan, scale 1:250.
   1 Eingang / Entrance
   2 Wohnraum / Lounge
   3 Eßplatz / Dining space
   4 Küche / Kitchen
   5 Fahrräder / Bicycles

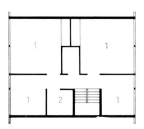

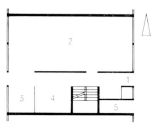

Reihenhäuser am Ørnegårdsvej, Jægersborg, Gentofte, 1957

Die für die Baufirma Jespersen & Søn errichteten Reihenhäuser haben zweigeschossige Wohnungen, deren tragende Querwände aus vorgefertigten Stahlbetontafeln bestehen. Die Curtain-Wall-Fassaden sind aus Holz mit Eternit-Füllungen.

Terrace houses at Ørnegårdsvej, Jægersborg, Gentofte, 1957

The terrace houses, erected for Messrs. Jespersen & Søn, Building Contractors, contain two-storey dwellings with bearing cross-walls consisting of pre-fabricated reinforced concrete slabs. The curtain wall façades are of wood, with asbestos cement infilling panels.

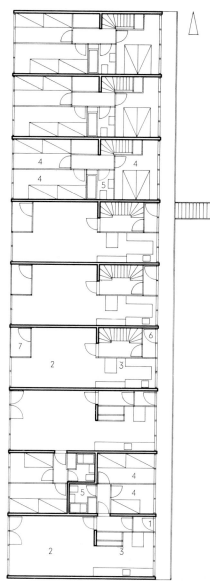

1 Ansicht von Südwesten auf die dem Rathaus von Rødovre (Seite 90) zugewandte Westfassade.
  View, from South-West, of the West front which faces Rødovre Town Hall (page 90).
2 Grundriß Erdgeschoß, 1. und 2. Obergeschoß M 1:250 / Plans of the ground floor and the first and second floor, scale 1:250.
  1 Eingang der eingeschossigen Wohnung
    Entrance to the single-storey dwelling
  2 Wohnraum / Lounge
  3 Küche / Kitchen
  4 Schlafzimmer / Bedrooms
  5 Bad und WC / Bathroom and W. C.
  6 Eingang der zweigeschossigen Wohnung im 1. Obergeschoß
    Entrance of the dwelling on the first floor, which extends through two storeys
  7 Balkon / Balcony

Wohnblock in Rødovre, 1960

Die zweigeschossigen oberen Wohnungen des langen Wohnblocks werden von einem Laubengang entlang der Ostseite erschlossen. Der Bau wurde mit vorgefertigten tragenden Stahlbeton-Querwänden errichtet, während die Fassaden als Curtain Walls aus Holz mit Eternit-Brüstungen ausgebildet sind. Der Laubengang besteht aus Stahlblechtafeln.

Block of dwellings at Rødovre, 1960

The upper dwellings of this long block extend through two storeys and are reached from an access balcony along the East side. The building has pre-fabricated load bearing reinforced concrete cross-walls, and curtain wall façades of wood with asbestos cement panels. The balcony consists of steel plates.

1 Ansicht von Osten (vom Øresund). Im Vordergrund die Badezelte des Bellevue-Strandes.
View from the East, i. e. from the Sound. In the foreground, the bathing tents of Bellevue Lido.
2 Lageplan M 1:2000.
Layout plan, scale 1:2000.
3 Ansicht des viergeschossigen Baus von Süden. Im Hintergrund die Bellavista-Appartements von 1933.
View of the four-storey block from the South. In the background, the Bellavista flats dating back to 1933.

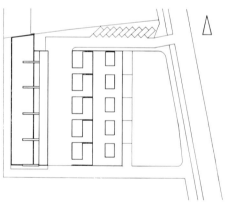

Wohnbebauung Bellevue Bugt, Klampenborg, Gentofte, 1960-61

Die neuen Wohnbauten wurden parallel zum Strandvej errichtet und sind den Bellevue-Appartements von 1933 unmittelbar benachbart. Sie bestehen aus einem viergeschossigen Wohnblock und fünf zum Sund hin vorgelagerten Atriumhäusern. Die durchlaufenden Balkonbrüstungen des mehrgeschossigen Wohnhauses, denen gegenüber die Vertikalen der schwarz gestrichenen, tragenden Querwände ganz zurücktreten, geben dem Gebäude eine starke horizontale Betonung. Die große Haustiefe von 20,30 m wurde für ein innenliegendes Kaminzimmer ausgenutzt. Das Erdgeschoß enthält Eingänge und Garagen.

Bellevue Bay Housing Estate, Klampenborg, Gentofte, 1960-61

The new buildings are parallel to the main road (Strandvej) and are immediately adjacent to the Bellavista flats built in 1933. They comprise a four-storey block and five atrium houses in front of the block, facing the Sound. The continuous balcony parapets of the multi-storey block, far more conspicuous than the vertical lines of the black-painted load-bearing cross-walls, strongly emphasize the horizontal orientation of the building. The great depth of the house, 20.30 metres (66½ ft.), has been utilized for a log fire lounge in the interior. The ground floor contains entrances and garages.

54

8 Ansicht der Atriumhäuser von Nordosten.
Der große Wohnraum besitzt ein Aussichtsfenster nach Osten auf den Øresund, wird aber außerdem wie das Eßzimmer, die Küche und das große Schlafzimmer vom Innenhof her belichtet. Die
nach Westen gelegenen Räume erhalten
ihr Licht von einem Gartenhof zwischen
Wohnhaus und Garagen.
View of the atrium house from North-
East. The large lounge has a picture
window facing the Sound in the East;
but, like the dining room, kitchen and
large bedroom, it also receives daylight
through the atrium. The rooms on the
West side receive their daylight from a
patio situated between the block of flats
and the garages.

9 Atriumhäuser. Grundriß M 1:400.
Atrium houses. Plan, scale 1:400.

   1 Garagen / Garages
   2 Gartenhof / Patio
   3 Eingang / Entrance
   4 Flur / Corridor
   5 Schlafzimmer / Bedrooms
   6 Bad / Bathroom
   7 WC
   8 Küche / Kitchen
   9 Abstellraum / Spare room
  10 Schrankzimmer / Storage room
  11 Eßzimmer / Dining room
  12 Wohnraum / Lounge

10 Blick in einen Innenhof.
   A view of the atrium.

Zentralschule, Hårby auf Fünen, 1951

Mit der Aufgliederung in klar abgegrenzte Baukörper aus Ziegelsteinmauerwerk paßte Jacobsen die Schulanlage dem Charakter des Dorfes an. Die gegeneinander versetzten Lehrerhäuser, das Hauptgebäude mit Aula und Normalklassen und ein Flügel mit Spezialklassen gruppieren sich um einen mit Gras bewachsenen Hof. Spielplatz und Pausenhof liegen auf der Südseite des Schulkomplexes.

Hårby Central School, Hårby, Funen, 1951

By arranging the accommodation in minor, clearly identifiable brick buildings, Jacobsen has adapted the school to the character of the village. The staggered row of terrace houses for teachers, the main building with assembly hall and standard classrooms and a wing with special classrooms are grouped around a lawn. Playground and schoolyard are on the South side of the group of buildings.

1 Ansicht von Nordwesten.
  View from the North-West.
2 Trinkbecken auf dem Spielplatz.
  Drinking fountain in the playground.

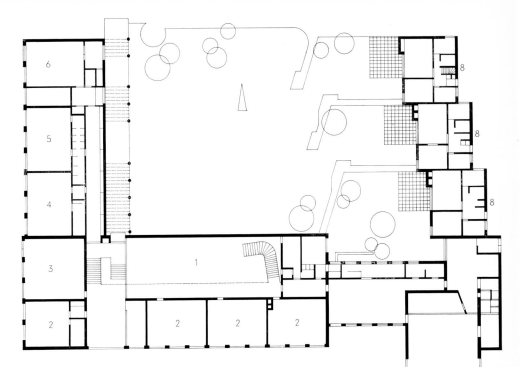

3 Grundriß Erdgeschoß M 1:500.
Ground floor plan, scale 1:500.
1 Aula / Assembly hall
2 Normalklassen / Standard classrooms
3 Bibliothek und Lesezimmer
  Library and reading room
4 Sonderklasse für Physikunterricht
  Physics laboratory
5 Werkraum / Crafts room
6 Schulküche / School kitchen
7 Turnhalle / Gymnasium
8 Lehrerwohnungen / Teachers' houses
4 Ansicht von Nordwesten mit Lehrerwohnungen und Hauptgebäude.
  View from North-West, with teachers'
  houses and main building.

5 Spielplatz und Pausenhof mit Hauptgebäude und Turnhalle.
  Playground and schoolyard, with main
  building and gymnasium.
6 Freitragende Stahlbetontreppe zum Balkon der Aula, der zugleich die Klassenräume des Obergeschosses erschließt.
  Free-standing reinforced concrete stairs
  leading to the assembly hall gallery which
  also gives access to the upper floor classrooms.
7 Aula. Das Haupttreppenhaus ist von der
  Aula durch eine Glaswand getrennt.
  Assembly hall. The main staircase is separated from the assembly hall by a glass
  partition.

58

◁ 3 Ansicht des zweigeschossigen Flügels mit den Spezialklassen von Norden. Die Klassenräume haben durchlaufende Ventilationsschlitze.
View from the North of the two-storey wing containing the special classrooms. These have a continuous ribbon of ventilation slits.

4 Wohnungen des Hausmeisters und des Inspektors. Ansicht von Osten.
Caretaker's and School Inspector's dwellings, seen from East.

5 Blick auf den östlichen Teil des Schulhofes.
Eastern part of schoolyard·

10 Trinkbrunnen auf dem Schulhof aus
   schwedischem Marmor.
   Drinking fountains in the schoolyard,
   made of Swedish marble.
11 Die Bepflanzung wechselt in jedem Gartenhof (siehe auch Seite 170). Im Hof der
   Kleinsten sind lustig beschnittene Büsche
   entstanden.
   Each of the patios has different vegetation (see page 170). That of the smallest
   children has gaily clipped shrubs.

12 Blick auf einen Teil der Schulanlage.
Part of the school complex.

16 Jacobsen hat selbst auch die gärtneri-
sche Gestaltung der ganzen Anlage fest-
gelegt und dabei jedem Gartenhof durch
die Art des Plattenbelags und die Wahl
der Bepflanzung einen besonderen Charakter gegeben. Statt der gewünschten
dekorativen Ausschmückung der Schule
entschied sich Jacobsen für die Anschaf-
fung einer großen Zahl von Abgüssen
klassischer und moderner Plastiken, die
in den Gartenhöfen aufgestellt wurden.
Jacobsen himself has directed the landscape gardening for the entire complex,
and has endowed each of the patios with
a character of its own, by choosing different flag paving and different vegetation. Instead of complying with a wish to
decorate the building itself, Jacobsen
decided to acquire a large number of
copies of classic and modern sculptures
which were erected in the patios.

17 Gehweg entlang der Ostseite der Klas-
senpavillons. Im Hintergrund die Turnhalle für die jüngeren Kinder.
Walkway along the East side of the
classroom pavilions, with the gymnasium
for younger children in the background.

◁ 18 Von den westlich gelegenen Gartenhöfen
führen Treppen mit Stufen aus vorgespanntem Beton zum Sportplatz.
From the patios on the West side, stairs
with prestressed concrete steps lead
down to the sports ground.

19 Ansicht der Turnhalle von Westen. Die
Treppe stellt die Verbindung zum Sportplatz her.
Gymnasium, seen from the West. The
stairs connect with the sports ground.

20 Ansicht der Schulanlage von Westen
(vom Sportplatz).
School buildings, seen from the West,
i.e. from the sports ground.

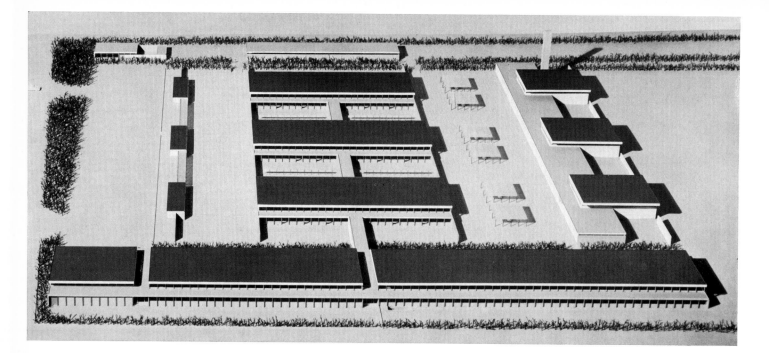

Schule, Rødovre, Entwurf 1959

1959 gewann Jacobsen den engeren Wettbewerb für eine neue Gemeindeschule in Rødovre, deren Baubeginn bevorsteht. Drei Klassentrakte nehmen je zwölf Normalklassen auf. Auf jeder Seite des Korridors, der die Flügel miteinander verbindet, liegen sechs Klassenräume. Sie werden durch Flure mit Oberlichtern erschlossen, die in der Längsachse der Gebäude verlaufen. Je drei Klassen von zwei gegenüberliegenden Flügeln haben einen gemeinsamen Gartenhof, der in der Mitte durch Blenden optisch geteilt ist, damit der Blick nicht in die gegenüberliegende Klasse fällt. Der lange Trakt mit den Spezialklassen an einem Mittelflur schließt die Anlage nach Westen ab. Südlich der Normalklassen befinden sich die Turnhallen, die über die flachen Zwischenbauten mit den Umkleideräumen hinausragen.

Rødovre School, Project, 1959

In 1959, Jacobsen won a limited design competition for a new council school at Rødovre, which is now about to be constructed. There will be three classroom wings, each containing twelve standard classrooms, viz. six on either side of the passage which connects the wings with each other. They are accessible through corridors with fanlights, which lie in the longitudinal centre lines of the buildings. Three classrooms in each of two opposing wings share a patio which is centrally divided by optical fences so that pupils cannot look into the classroom on the opposite side. The long wing with the special classrooms, accessible from a central corridor, forms the Western outpost of the school. To the South of the standard classrooms are the gymnasia which rise above the low annexes containing the changing rooms.

1 Modellansicht von Westen.
  Model, seen from the West.
2 Grundriß M 1:1000.
  Plan, scale 1:1000.
3 Modellansicht von Süden.
  Model, seen from the South.

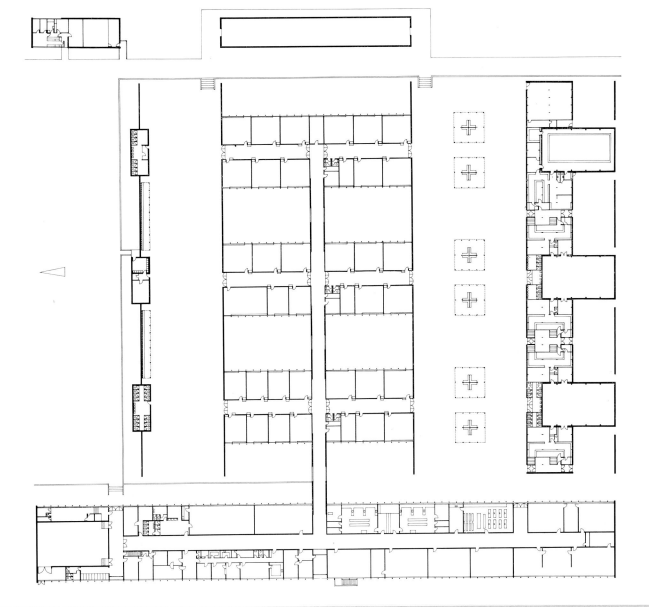

1 Modellansicht von oben.
  Model seen from above.

St. Catherine's College, Oxford, Entwurf 1960

Die streng konzipierte Anlage liegt verhältnismäßig isoliert von der Stadt auf einem flachen Wiesengelände am Fluß. In den beiden langen dreigeschossigen Trakten sind in den Obergeschossen die Wohnschlafräume der Schüler untergebracht, während sich die Lehrerwohnungen im Erdgeschoß befinden. Die parallelen Wohnflügel umschließen einen Platz, auf dessen nördlicher Hälfte Speisesaal mit dazu gehörigen Gesellschaftsräumen, Küche und Wirtschaftsräume liegen. Im Süden werden Bibliothek, Glockenturm und Auditorium errichtet. Das Haus des Rektors liegt auf einem dreieckigen Grundstück am Fluß.

St. Catherine's College, Oxford, Project, 1960

The strictly conceived group of buildings lies in a somewhat isolated position on a flat riverside meadow. The two long three-storey blocks contain, on the upper floors, the bed-sitting rooms of the undergraduates whilst the tutors' flats are on the ground floor. The parallel blocks lie on opposite sides of a square which is otherwise occupied, in the northern part, by the dining hall with its common rooms, kitchen and utility rooms and, in the South, by a library, bell-tower and an assembly hall. The Master's house will be built on a triangular site near the river.

3 Modellansicht von Süden. Zwischen Fluß ▷ und westlichem Wohntrakt befindet sich eine Gartenanlage mit geschützten und sonnigen Leseplätzen entlang eines langgestreckten Wasserbassins.
Model, seen from the South. Between river and West Block, there is a garden with protected and sunny reading places along a long and narrow pool of water.

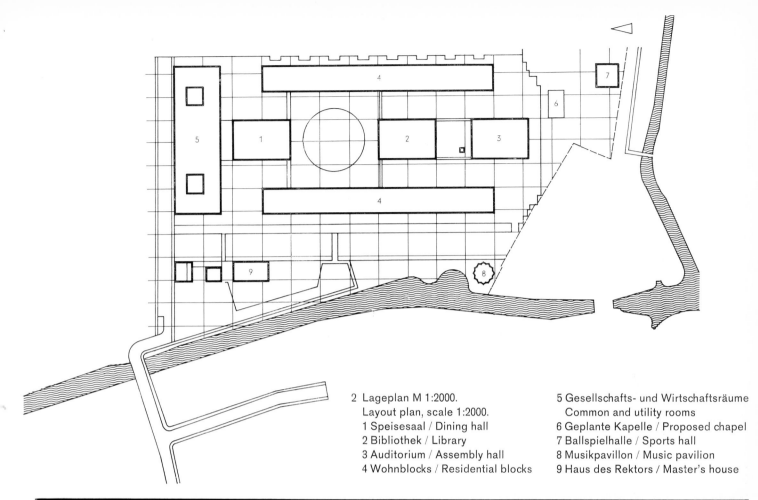

2 Lageplan M 1:2000.
  Layout plan, scale 1:2000.
  1 Speisesaal / Dining hall
  2 Bibliothek / Library
  3 Auditorium / Assembly hall
  4 Wohnblocks / Residential blocks

5 Gesellschafts- und Wirtschaftsräume
  Common and utility rooms
6 Geplante Kapelle / Proposed chapel
7 Ballspielhalle / Sports hall
8 Musikpavillon / Music pavilion
9 Haus des Rektors / Master's house

4 Wohnhaus des Rektors am Fluß. Modellansicht von Süden.
  Master's House at the river bank. Model,
  seen from the South.
5 Der westliche Wohntrakt mit einem Musikpavillon am Fluß. Modellansicht von Nordwesten.
  West Block with riverside music pavilion.
  Model, seen from North-West.

6 Modellansicht von Osten. Der östliche
Wohntrakt fehlt bei dieser Aufnahme.
Model, seen from the East. In this photo-
graph, the East Block has been omitted.

7 Modellansicht von Westen. Die Konstruktion der Wohnflügel beruht auf tragenden Stahlbeton-Wandscheiben. Die Stirnwände sind aus gelben Ziegelsteinen.
Model, seen from the West. The structure
of the residential block rests on load-
bearing reinforced concrete wall slabs.
The end walls are of yellow brick.

Tennishalle des Sportklubs Hellerup, Hartmannsvej, Gentofte, 1935

Stahlbetonrippen mit Dachpappe bilden das halbtonnenförmige Dach. Die Stirnwände und der zugehörige Bau mit den Umkleideräumen sind in gelbem Backsteinmauerwerk ausgeführt. Der Südgiebel ist, wie der Architekt es beabsichtigt hatte, mit Kletterpflanzen zugewachsen.

Tennis Hall of Hellerup Sports Club, Hartmannsvej, Gentofte, 1935

The barrel roof is formed by reinforced concrete arches and roofing felt. The end walls and the changing rooms annex are of yellow brickwork. The South wall is now covered by climbers as was intended by the architect.

1 Ansicht von Süden.
  View from the South.
2 Innenansicht.
  Interior.

Gentofte-Stadion, Jægersborg, Gentofte, 1941-42

Die Anlage wurde nach Plänen ausgeführt, mit denen Arne Jacobsen 1936 einen engeren Wettbewerb gewonnen hatte. Die Materialbeschränkungen der Kriegszeit wirkten sich aus; die Bauten aus rotem Backsteinmauerwerk zeigen nur kleine Fensteröffnungen, die mit traditionellen Fensterstürzen überdeckt werden konnten.

Gentofte Stadium, Jægersborg, Gentofte, 1941-42

The stadium was constructed in accordance with plans which had, in 1936, gained for Arne Jacobsen the First Prize in a limited design competition. The wartime shortages of building materials are apparent; the red brick buildings have window openings small enough to be covered by conventional lintels.

Segelboothafen, Vejle, Entwurf 1949

Als Bauplatz war eine kleine bewaldete Landspitze in einer beliebten Ausflugsgegend am Vejle Fjord vorgesehen. Das Projekt umfaßt neben der Hafenanlage für Segel-, Renn- und Motorboote ein Schützenhaus, ein Klubgebäude und ein Restaurant. Jacobsen errang mit diesem Entwurf, der nicht realisiert worden ist, in einem Wettbewerb den ersten Preis.

Yacht Harbour, Vejle, Project, 1949

The site envisaged for this project was a small wooded peninsula at a popular beauty spot at Vejle Fjord. In addition to the harbour for yachts, speed boats and motor boats, the project comprises a rifle club, a club building and a restaurant. With this project, which was not carried out, Jacobsen had won the First Prize in a design competition.

1 Ansichten des Restaurants von Norden und Westen.
Views of the restaurant from the North and from the West.
2 Lageplan M 1:4000.
Layout plan, scale 1:4000.

Sporthalle, Landskrona, Entwurf 1956

Die Konstruktion der Halle ermöglichte große schräge Fensterpartien, die nach Bedarf durch Lamellen abgeschirmt werden sollten. Das Wettbewerbsprojekt Jacobsens, das 1956 den ersten Preis erhielt und auch ein Rathaus und eine Bibliothek umfaßte, wurde zugunsten eines neuen Vorschlages (Seite 84) aufgeben.

Landskrona Sports Hall, Project, 1956

The design of the hall permitted the provision af large inclined windows which were to be screened by slats as required. Jacobsen's competition project which was awarded the First Prize in 1956 and which also comprised a town hall and a library, was later abandoned in favour of a new project (page 84).

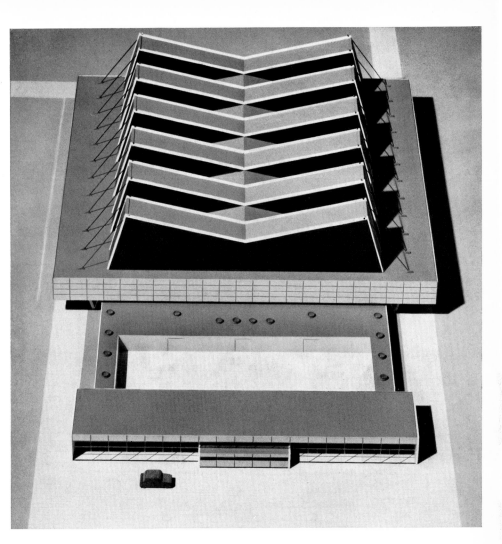

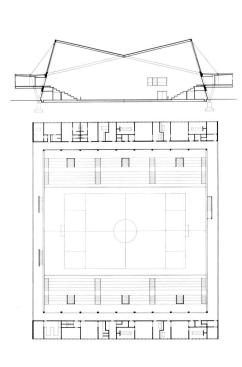

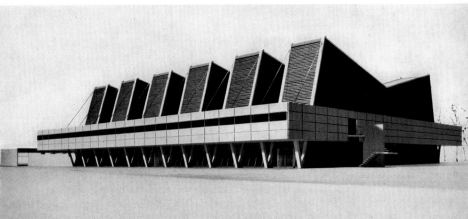

1 Schnitt M 1:1000.
   Section, scale 1:1000.
2 Modellansicht von Süden.
   Model, seen from the South.
3 Grundriß M 1:1000.
   Plan, scale 1:1000.
4 Modellansicht von Nordosten.
   Model, seen from the North-East.

9 Detail der schwarzen Steinplatten-Ver-
blendung an der Längsseite des Sitzungs-
gebäudes mit dem Stadtwappen von Rødovre. Im Hintergrund ist das Hauptgebäude sichtbar.
Details of the black stone-slab cladding
on the long side of the Council Chamber
building with the Rødovre coat-of-arms.
In the background the main building.

▷

10 Detail des Curtain Walls am Hauptgebäude. Die Sprossen sind mit Profilen
aus rostfreiem Stahl verkleidet.
Detail of the curtain wall of the main
building. The curtain wall bars are covered with stainless steel sections.

15 Büro des Bürgermeisters. Wände und
Schrankfächer sind mit verschiedenen
Hölzern furniert. Alle Trennwände des
Büroflügels sind, entsprechend dem
1-Meter-Modul der Fassade, versetzbar
und bestehen aus einer Pfostenkon-
struktion mit Füllungen aus schallschluk-
kenden Svedex-Elementen.

Mayor's Parlour. Walls and cupboards
are veneered with different species of
wood. All the partitions in the office
wing, which correspond to the 1 metre
module of the façade, are movable and
consist of a stanchion framework with
infilling panels of sound-absorbing "Sve-
dex" units.

16 Das Trauzimmer ist mit Arne Jacobsens
Serienstühlen eingerichtet.
The Registrar's Office is furnished with
series-produced chairs of Arne Jacobsen's design.

17 Büroraum mit Möbeln aus Teakholz.
Office room with teakwood furniture.

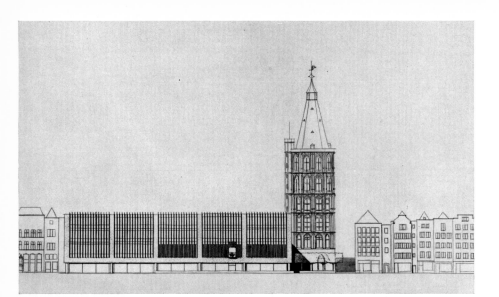

Rathauserweiterung, Köln, Entwurf 1958

1 Ansicht von Osten.
2 Modellansicht von Westen.
3 Lageplan M 1:1500.

**Extension of Cologne Town Hall,
Project, 1958**

1 View from the East.
2 Model, seen from the West.
3 Layout plan, scale 1:1500.

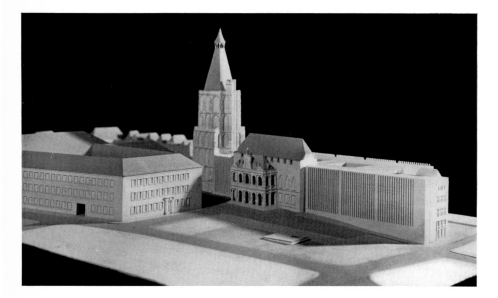

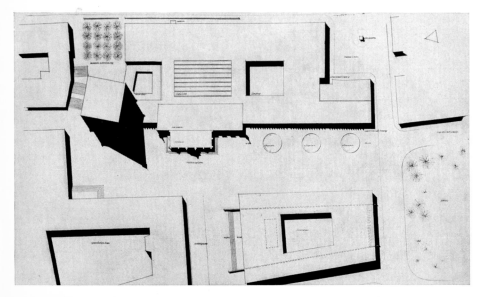

Rathaus, Marl, Entwurf 1957

Jacobsen gliederte den Komplex in einen hohen Querriegel, der die Verwaltungsbehörden der fünf Stadtdezernate aufnehmen sollte, und in einen quadratischen Baukörper mit verschiedenen Sälen, der als repräsentativer Teil des Rathauses gedacht war. Nach Südwesten schließt sich das — ebenfalls ausgeschriebene — Polizeigebäude an. Der Entwurf, der in einem engeren Wettbewerb entstand, wurde angekauft.

Marl Town Hall, Germany, Project, 1957

Jacobsen's design envisaged a high transverse block for the offices of the five municipal departments, and a square building with a number of large rooms intended to form the representative part of the town hall. Connected to it on the South-West side was the police headquarters building which was also included in the limited competition. The design was bought.

1 Ansicht von Nordwesten.
   View from North-West.
2 Lageplan.
   Layout plan.

Wettbewerbsentwurf für das Rathaus in Essen, 1962

Das Projekt sieht vor, das vorhandene Grundstück in seiner ganzen Ausdehnung mit einem Flachbausockel zu überbauen, über dem sich ein in Nord-Süd-Richtung orientiertes Hochhaus erhebt. Zwei Kellergeschosse mit einbahnigen Auf- und Abfahrten und das Einfahrtgeschoß bieten Parkmöglichkeiten für 1100 Wagen. Eine kreisförmige Rampe führt auf die (normalerweise dem Fußgänger vorbehaltene) Plattform des Eingangsgeschosses hinauf. Von dieser platzartigen Terrasse aus erreicht man die zentrale Halle, die von den beiden Hauptaufzugsgruppen flankiert wird. Weitere Aufzüge in den beiden äußeren Türmen des Hochhauses dienen dem internen Verkehr. Die drei Hochhausteile sind durch die Aufzugsvorhallen miteinander verbunden. Die Fahrstühle selbst werden zusammen mit den Toiletten, den Feuertreppen und den Installationsschächten in Stahlbetontürmen zusammengefaßt, die am Außenbau als querlaufende Scheiben in Erscheinung treten. Zwischen diesen Türmen spannen sich im Bereich der Büroetagen geschoßhohe, vorgefertigte und vorgespannte Kastenträger, an denen jeweils die Kragträger für zwei Bürogeschosse montiert sind.

Competition project for Essen Town Hall, Germany, 1962

According to the project, the whole of the site will be covered by a low building which will be over-towered by a multi-storey block in north-south orientation. Two basements with single-lane down and up ramps, together with the entrance floor, will offer parking facilities for 1100 cars within convenient walking distance to the lifts. A circular ramp will lead up to the entrance floor forecourt, normally reserved for pedestrians. This high-level piazza provides access to the central entrance hall with its information counter and display area, flanked by the two main batteries of lifts. Further lifts in the two tower blocks on either side will serve internal traffic. The three tower blocks will be connected across the lift landings. Lifts, lavatories, emergency stairs, installation shafts and air-conditioning ducts are concentrated in reinforced concrete towers which appear, on the outside, as transverse piers. Between these towers, the office floors are supported by storey-high prefabricated and prestressed box girders, each of them carrying the cantilever beams for two floors.

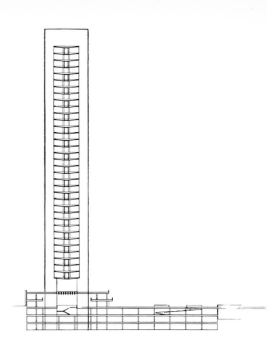

1 Schnitt durch Hochhaus und Sockelzone M 1:2000.
Cross-section of tower block and low building, scale 1:2000.
2 Modellansicht von Nordwesten.
Model, seen from North-West.

3 Modellansicht von Westen mit umliegen-
  der Bebauung.
  Model, seen from the West, with surround-
  ing buildings.
4 Grundriß des obersten Sockelgeschosses
  M 1:2000.
  Plan of the top floor of the low building,
  scale 1:2000.
5 Grundriß des Eingangsgeschosses
  M 1:2000.
  Plan of entrance floor, scale 1:2000.
6 Grundriß des unteren Kellergeschosses
  M 1:2000.
  Plan of lower basement, scale 1:2000.

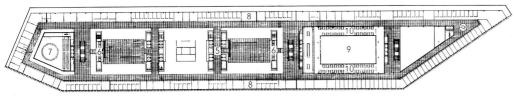

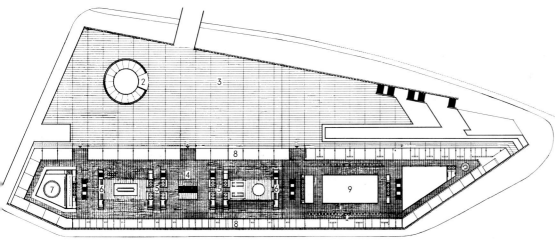

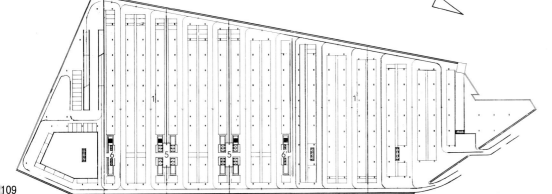

Legende zu den Plänen
Key to plans
1 Parkstände / Parking stalls
2 Rampe zum Rathaus-Vorplatz
  Ramp leading to the town
  hall forecourt
3 Fußgängerzone (Rathaus-
  Vorplatz)
  Pedestrian zone (town hall
  forecourt)
4 Eingangshalle / Entrance hall
5 Hauptaufzugsgruppen
  Main lift batteries
6 Interne Aufzüge
  Lifts for internal traffic
7 Kleiner Sitzungssaal
  Small Council Chamber
8 Büroräume / Offices
9 Luftraum Wirtschaftshof
  Air space above the service
  courtyard
10 Kantine / Canteen

Ausstellungsgebäude und Ersatzteillager Massey-Harris, Roskildevej, Glostrup, 1952

Die voll verglaste Längsseite der Ausstellungshalle liegt zur Landstraße hin, so daß die aufgestellten Fabrikate der Landmaschinenfabrik weithin sichtbar sind. Im Westen schließt sich ein niedriger Büroflügel an. Die Konstruktion des Bauwerks besteht aus einem System von Stahlbetonstützen und -trägern, über denen Betontafeln das Dach bilden. Die Außenmauern sind aus gelbem Backstein. Auf der Internationalen Architekturausstellung in São Paulo erhielt das Gebäude eine Auszeichnung.

Massey-Harris Display Room and Spares Depot, Roskildevej, Glostrup, 1952

The completely glazed front of the display room faces the highway so that the agricultural machines produced and displayed by this company are visible from a great distance. On the West side is a low office annex. The structure of the building consists of a system of reinforced concrete stanchions and beams, roofed with concrete slabs. The outer walls are of yellow brick. The design obtained a Citation at the International Architectural Exhibition at São Paulo.

1 Ansicht der Ausstellungshalle von Norden.
  View of display room from the North.
2 Innenansicht der Ausstellungshalle.
  Interior of display room.
3 Der beleuchtete Ausstellungsraum bei Nacht.
  The lit-up display room at night.
4 Grundriß M 1:1000 / Plan, scale 1:1000.
  1 Ausstellungshalle / Display room
  2 Büroräume / Offices
  3 Ersatzteillager / Spares depot
  4 Lagerraum für Maschinen / Machinery stores
  5 Werkstatt / Workshop
5 Teilansicht der Halle. Eine leichte Treppe mit frei auskragenden Betonstufen führt zu einem Werkstattbüro.
  Partial view of display room. A lightly constructed flight of stairs with cantilevered concrete steps leads to a workshop office.

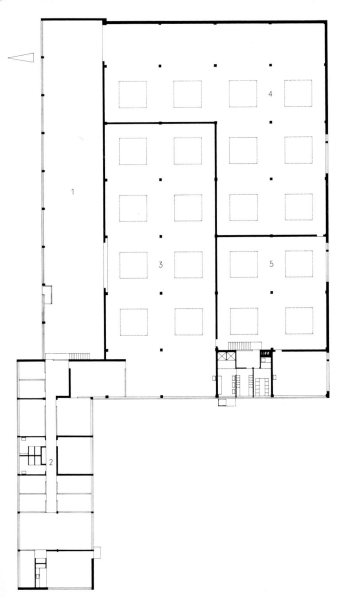

Fabrikanlage Carl Christensen, Ålborg, 1956

Die Fabrik liegt parallel zu einer Hauptstraße südlich von Ålborg. Der Komplex besteht aus einer nach Osten orientierten Fabrikhalle mit Nebenräumen, die nach Westen gehen, und einem vorgelagerten kleineren Bürotrakt. Der Bau wurde als Stahlbeton-Skelettkonstruktion errichtet. Stirnseiten und Brüstungen sind aus Mauerwerk.

Carl Christensen's Factory, Ålborg, 1956

The factory faces a main road to the South of Ålborg. The group of buildings consists of a factory hall, which has an East orientation, with ancillary premises facing West, and a small office annex in front of it. The building has a framework structure of reinforced concrete. End walls and parapets are of brick.

112

1 Ansicht von Osten (Hauptansicht).
  View from the East (main frontage).
2 Ansicht von Norden entlang der Hauptfassade.
  View from the North, along the main
  frontage.
3 Grundriß M 1:500.
  Plan, scale 1:500.
4 Ansicht von Süden.
  View from the South.

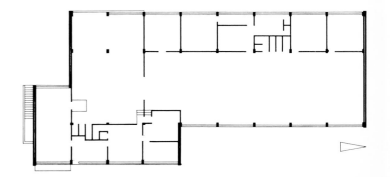

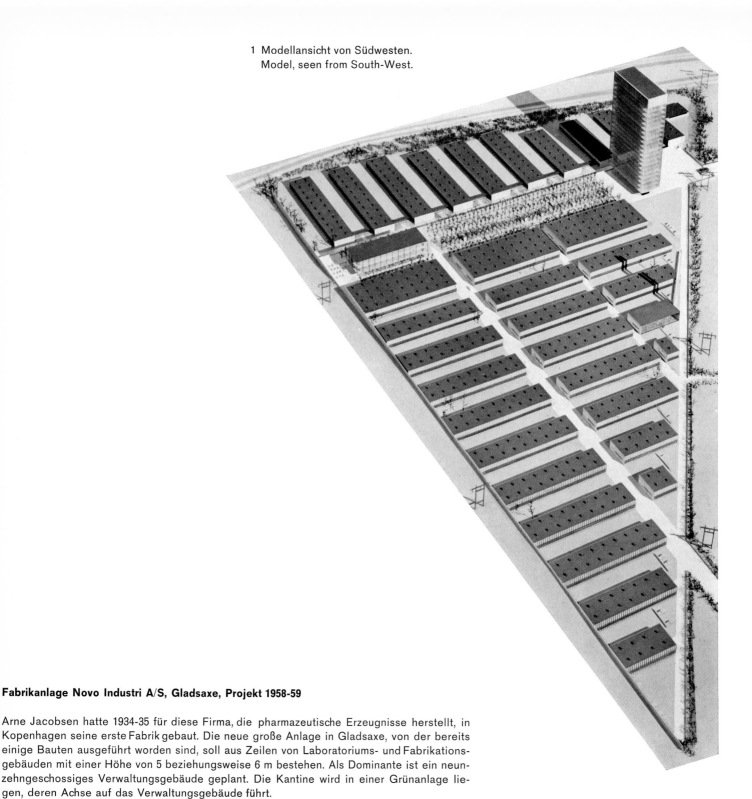

Fabrikanlage Novo Industri A/S, Gladsaxe, Projekt 1958-59

Arne Jacobsen hatte 1934-35 für diese Firma, die pharmazeutische Erzeugnisse herstellt, in Kopenhagen seine erste Fabrik gebaut. Die neue große Anlage in Gladsaxe, von der bereits einige Bauten ausgeführt worden sind, soll aus Zeilen von Laboratoriums- und Fabrikations-gebäuden mit einer Höhe von 5 beziehungsweise 6 m bestehen. Als Dominante ist ein neunzehngeschossiges Verwaltungsgebäude geplant. Die Kantine wird in einer Grünanlage liegen, deren Achse auf das Verwaltungsgebäude führt.

Novo Industri A/S Factory, Gladsaxe, Project, 1958-59

In 1934-35, Arne Jacobsen had built his first factory, in Copenhagen, for this company which manufactures pharmaceutical products. The new large plant at Gladsaxe, where some of the buildings already stand, will consist of rows of laboratory and factory buildings of a height of 5 and 6 metres (16′5″ and 19′8″) respectively. The plant will be dominated by a 19-storey office block. The canteen will come to lie in a park orientated towards the office block.

2 Modellansicht von Norden.
  Model, seen from the North.
3 Modellansicht von Osten.
  Model, seen from the East.

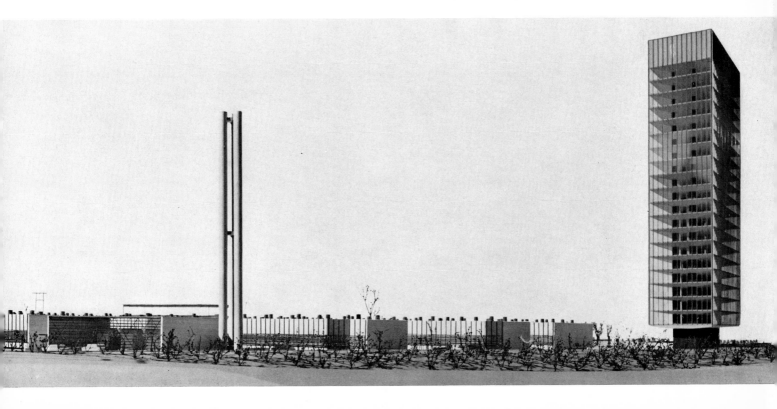

Fabrikbau Novo Industri A/S, Hillerødgade, Kopenhagen, 1961

Der Neubau für das Kopenhagener Zweigwerk der Novo Industri, eine Fabrik für Gärstoffe, wurde als Stahlbetonkonstruktion mit verstellbaren Aluminiumlamellen vor den Fenstern des Erdgeschosses errichtet. Die außenliegende Nottreppe ist von einem Zylinder aus Stahl und Glas umschlossen.

Novo Industri A/S Factory, Hillerødgade, Copenhagen, 1961

The new building for the Copenhagen branch of Novo Industri A/S, a ferments factory, was erected in reinforced concrete, with adjustable aluminium slats covering the ground floor windows. The external emergency staircase is enclosed by a cylinder of steel and glass.

Bürogebäude Jespersen & Søn, Kopenhagen, 1955

Die vertikalen Tragelemente des Gebäudes bestehen aus zwei massiven Stahlbetonpfeilern, die sich im ersten Obergeschoß in je ein Stützenpaar gabeln. Die Decken werden von zwei Längsunterzügen getragen. Zwischen den Stützenpaaren verläuft der Mittelkorridor der zwei-bündigen Anlage. An die Vorderkanten der weit auskragenden Geschoßplatten ist die Fassade, ein reiner Curtain Wall, angeschlossen. Die Ostseite gegen die Nyropsgade hat fest verglaste Fenster in aluminiumverkleideten Holzrahmen, die Hofseite Wendeflügel mit Thermoglasscheiben. Das ganze Erdgeschoß ist offen und als Durchfahrt ausgebildet.

Office block for Messrs. Jespersen & Søn, Copenhagen, 1955

The vertical bearing elements of the structure consist of two massive reinforced concrete columns each of which bifurcates, at first floor level, into a pair of stanchions. The floors are carried by two strong longitudinal beams. Between the pair of stanchions runs the centre corridor. The front edges of the widely cantilevered structural floor slabs carry the curtain wall façade. On the East side, facing Nyropsgade, are permanently closed windows in aluminium-clad wooden frames; the windows on the courtyard side are pivoted and have thermoglass panes. The entire ground floor is kept free and serves as a passage.

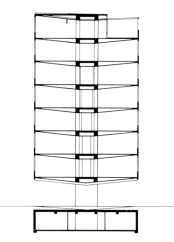

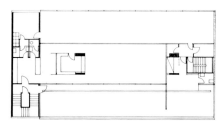

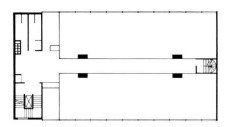

2 Ansicht von Südosten.
  View from South-East.
3 Schnitt M 1:500.
  Section, scale 1:500.
4 Grundriß 7. Obergeschoß M 1:500.
  7th floor plan, scale 1:500.
5 Grundriß Normalgeschoß M 1:500.
  Typical floor plan, scale 1:500.
6 Grundriß Erdgeschoß M 1:500.
  Ground floor plan, scale 1:500.

7 Die elegante verglaste Nottreppe in der Durchfahrt. Das Haupttreppenhaus befindet sich in dem bis zum Erdgeschoß durchgeführten Festpunkt.
The elegantly glazed emergency staircase in the passage. The main staircase is located in the "fixed point", carried down to ground level.

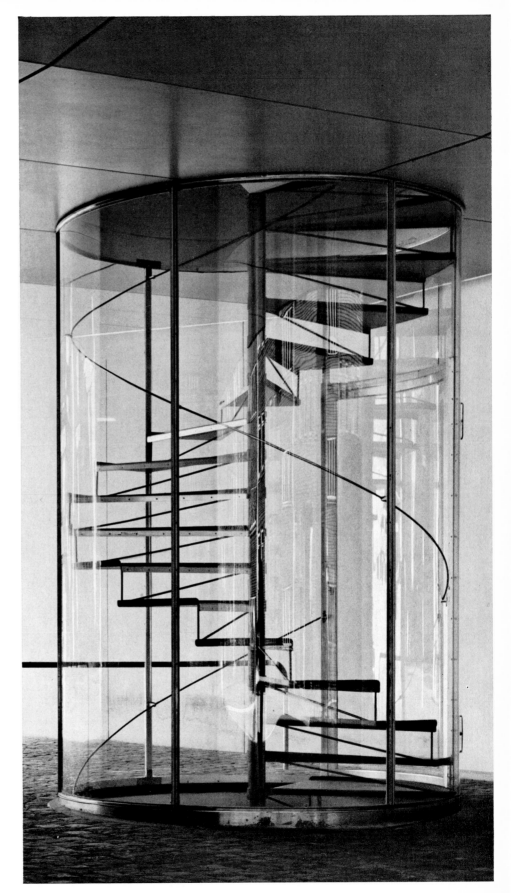

SAS-Hotel Royal und -Empfangsgebäude, Kopenhagen, 1958-60

Das Gebäude im Zentrum der Stadt dient nicht nur als Hotel, sondern auch als innerstädtisches Empfangsgebäude der SAS. Die Anlage gliedert sich in einen langen zweigeschossigen Bau, dessen Fensterband die Horizontale betont, und in einen Hotelturm, der sich frei über dem niedrigen Baukörper erhebt. Der flache Trakt nimmt in seinem nördlichen Teil die Abfertigungshalle der SAS, in seiner südlichen Hälfte Restaurant und Foyer des Hotels Royal auf; er ist mit dunklen, graugrün emaillierten Stahltafeln verkleidet. Das achtzehngeschossige Hochhaus — wie der Flachbau eine Stahlbetonkonstruktion — hat einen Curtain Wall aus dünnen, grau eloxierten Aluminiumprofilen mit Brüstungselementen aus graugrünem Glas.

SAS Hotel Royal and Air Terminal, Copenhagen, 1958-60

The building, situated in the town centre, comprises an hotel as well as an air terminal for the SAS. It is divided into a long two-storey block with a ribbon of windows emphasizing the horizontal line, and a multi-storey hotel tower which freely rises above the low building. The northern part of the low block houses the SAS terminal offices whilst its southern part contains the restaurant and foyer of the Hotel Royal; it has a cladding of dark, grey-green enamelled steel plates. The 18-storey tower block which, like the low building, has a reinforced concrete framework, has a curtain wall of thin, grey anodized aluminium sections with grey-green glass panels.

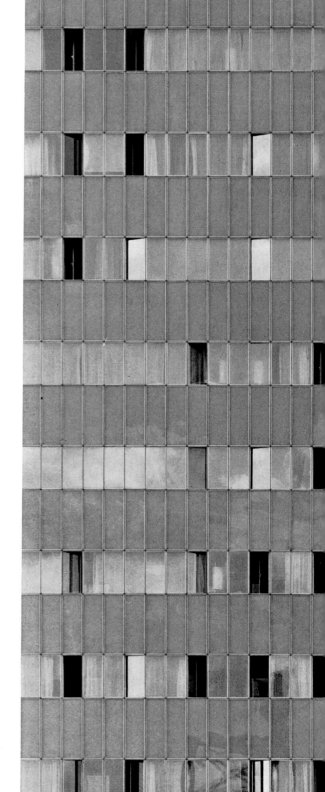

1 Fassadenausschnitt des Hochhauses.
Details of tower block façade.

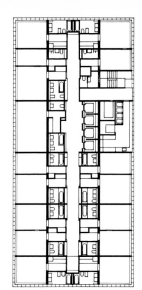

2 Grundriß Hoteletage M ca. 1:500.
 Hotel floor plan, scale 1:500.
3 Grundriß 1. Obergeschoß M ca. 1:500.
 First floor plan, scale 1:500.
  1 Bar
  2 Büroräume / Offices
  3 Kantine / Canteen
  4 Sitzungssaal / Conference room
  5 Aufgang vom Foyer
   Stairs leading to the foyer
  6 Vestibül / Vestibule
  7 Aufenthalts- und Gesellschaftsräume
   Lounges and social rooms
  8 Restaurant
  9 Fahrstühle / Lifts
  10 Küchenräume / Kitchen premises

4 Grundriß Erdgeschoß M ca. 1:500.
 Ground floor plan, scale 1:500.
  1 Eingang zum Empfangsgebäude
   Entrance to air terminal
  2 Ausgang / Exit
  3 Abfahrt / Departure
  4 Ankunft / Arrival
  5 Wartesaal und Schalter
   Waiting room and counters
  6 Reisebüro und Kasse
   Travel Bureau and Cashier
  7 Eingang zum Hotel / Hotel entrance
  8 Hotelfoyer / Hotel foyer
  9 Aufgang zum Restaurant
   Stairs leading to restaurant
  10 Fahrstühle / Lifts
  11 Snackbar
  12 Wintergarten / Conservatory
  13 Konditorei / Tea room
  14 Läden / Shops

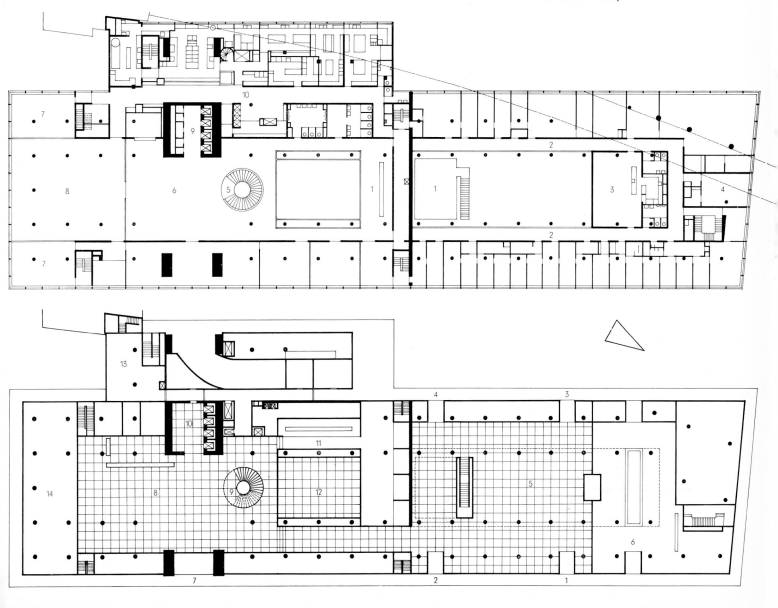

5 Ansicht von Süden.
  View from the South.
6 Ansicht von Nordwesten (von der Vester-
  brogade).
  View from North-West, i. e. from Vester-
  brogade.

7 Detail der Beleuchtung über dem Emp-
fangsschalter.
Light fittings above the reception counter.
8 Empfang. Der Schalter ist mit Wengé-
Holz furniert.
Reception counter, veneered with
Wengé wood.

9 Das Hotelfoyer ist auf zwei Seiten von Läden umschlossen, die sowohl von der Halle als auch von der Straße her betreten werden können. Tageslicht fällt durch den Haupteingang und den an das Foyer anschließenden Wintergarten ein. Der Boden ist mit hellgrauen Marmorplatten verlegt, die Decke wurde dunkelgrün gespritzt. Sämtliche Möbel sind von Jacobsen entworfen.

The hotel foyer is flanked on two sides by shops which can be entered from the hall as well as from the street. Daylight enters through the main entrance and through the conservatory adjacent to the foyer. The flooring consists of pale-grey marble slabs, the ceiling is sprayed in dark-green oil paint. All the furniture is designed by Arne Jacobsen.

10 Die Wendeltreppe zwischen Foyer und Restaurantgeschoß ist an Rundeisen aufgehängt. Die aus Stahlplatten zusammengeschweißten Treppenstufen sind mit einem dunkelgrünen Läufer belegt. Die Geländerfüllungen bestehen aus rauchfarbenem Plexiglas.
The spiral staircase between foyer and restaurant floor is suspended from steel rods. The steps, consisting of weld-assembled steel plates, have dark-green carpeting. Their side protection consists of smoke-coloured Plexiglass.

11 Vestibül des Restaurants. Möbel, Teppich ▷ und Lampen sind von Arne Jacobsen entworfen.
Restaurant vestibule, with furniture, carpet and lamps designed by Arne Jacobsen.

12 Vorraum mit den zu einer Gruppe zusammengefaßten Aufzügen vor dem Vestibül des Restaurants.
Lift landing at the restaurant vestibule.

13 An das Hotelfoyer schließt der zwei Geschoß hohe Wintergarten an. Zwischen
   den doppelten Glaswänden sind Orchi-
   deen aufgehängt. Hinter der Glaswand
   wird die Snackbar sichtbar.
   Adjacent to the hotel foyer is the two-
   storey high conservatory. It has double
   glass walls, with orchids suspended between them. Behind the glass wall, the
   snack bar can be seen.

14 Bar im 1. Obergeschoß mit Wandtäfelung
   aus Rosenholz, der Bartheke aus Bronze
   und Lampen aus rauchfarbenem Plexiglas. Die Sitzmöbel sind mit olivgrünem
   Wollstoff bezogen.
   First floor bar, with rosewood wall panelling, bronze bar counter, and lamps of
   smoke-coloured Plexiglass. The seats
   have an olive-green worsted covering.

15 Das Restaurant erhält Tages- und künst-
liches Licht durch die kreisrunden Glaskuppeln mit rauchfarbenen Glasglocken,
die das Licht brechen. Der Teppich, der
mit Goldfäden durchwirkte Wandbehang
und die Gardine zwischen Restaurant
und Vestibül haben dasselbe Muster.
The restaurant receives both day-light
and artificial light through the circular
domes. They contain suspended smoke-
coloured glass cups, refracting the light.
The carpet, the curtain shot with gold
thread, and the curtain between restaurant and vestibule show the same chess-
board pattern.

16 Die Glaskuppeln des Restaurants, vom
Hochhaus gesehen.
The glass domes of the restaurant, seen
from the tower block.

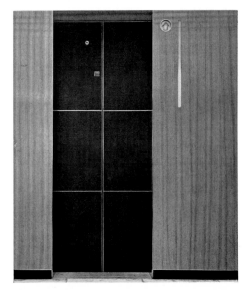

17 Nische in einem Gang vor den Hotelzimmern mit lederbezogenem Sessel von Jacobsen. Im Hintergrund ein polynesischer Rindenteppich.
Recess in a hotel corridor, with leather-covered armchair designed by Jacobsen. In the background, a tapistry of Polynesian bark.

18, 19 Türen und Wände der Aufzüge sind mit Wengé-Holz furniert, die Wandtäfelung des Vorraums besteht aus heller Eiche.
Lift doors and walls are veneered with Wengé wood; the wall panelling of the hall consists of light oak.

20-22 In allen Hotelzimmern sind die Holztäfelungen und das feste Inventar mit Wengé-Holz furniert. An der Wand sind Schubladenelemente befestigt, von denen eines als Frisiertoilette ausgebildet ist, ein anderes ist mit Bedienungsknöpfen für Rufanlage, Radio und Licht versehen. Die Lampen über den Wandelementen gleiten in verdeckten Schienen. Tischflächen sind mit graublauem Formica belegt. Der Schlafteil kann durch Vorhänge abgetrennt werden. Teil der Einrichtung ist Jacobsens Sessel »Das Ei«.

All the panelling and fixed furniture in the hotel rooms is veneered with Wengé wood. Drawer units are mounted on the wall; one of them is designed as a dressing table, another is provided with push buttons for staff, and for wireless and lighting. The lamps above the wall units can slide on covered rails so that they can be shifted as required. All table tops are of grey-blue Formica. The bedroom part can be curtained off from the rest of the room. Among the furniture is Jacobsen's armchair known as "The Egg".

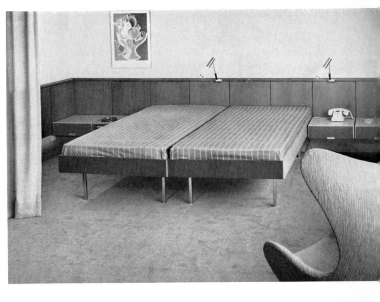

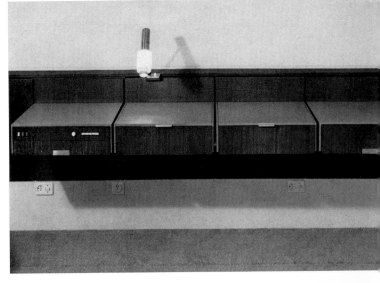

23 Telefonboxen. Blenden aus vorgespanntem Glas und Tischplatten aus Stahl.
   Public telephones with side screens of
   prestressed glass and desks of steel.
24 Treppe zum Balkon mit der Cafeteria.
   Stairs leading to upper floor cafeteria.
25 Schaltertisch des Reisebüros.
   Travel Bureau counter.

26 Die Gepäckabfertigung an der Längswand
   der Halle. Die Wandverkleidung ist aus
   Esche, die Kofferablage aus rostfreiem
   Stahl.
   Luggage section on the long side of the
   hall. The wall panelling consists of ash
   wood, the luggage counter of stainless
   steel.

27 Der zweigeschossige Wartesaal der SAS.
Die Treppen im Vordergrund führen zu
einer Cafeteria im Obergeschoß und zu
den Toiletten im Untergeschoß.
Two-storey waiting room for the SAS.
The stairs in the foreground lead to the
first floor cafeteria and to the cloakrooms
in the basement.

28 Trennwand in der Halle. Das leichte Stahl-
skelett hat Füllungen aus Glas und mit
Esche furnierten Holztafeln. Die Boden-
leiste besteht aus rostfreiem Stahl.
Panel wall in the hall. The light steel framework has panels of glass and wood,
which are veneered with ash wood. The
kick plate consists of stainless steel.

Verwaltungsgebäude Onderlinges, Den Haag, Entwurf 1959

Onderlinges' Headquarters Building, The Hague, Project, 1959

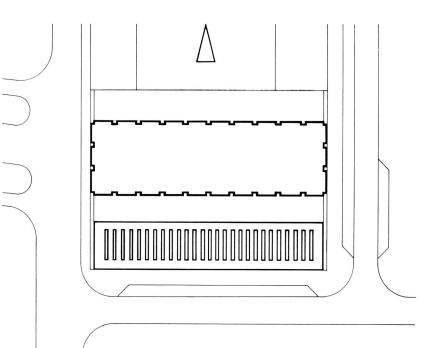

1 Ansicht von Süden. Die Flachbauten mit
  Oberlicht sind für den Publikumsverkehr
  bestimmt.
  View from the South. The low buildings
  with fanlights are to be open to the public.
2 Lageplan M 1:1000.
  Layout plan, scale 1:1000.

3 Ansicht von Westen.
  View from the West.
4 Grundriß Normalgeschoß M 1:500.
  Typical floor plan, scale 1:500.

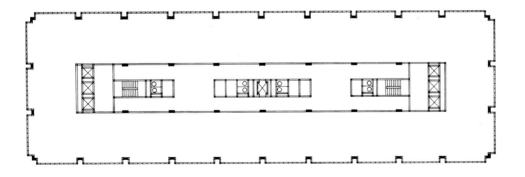

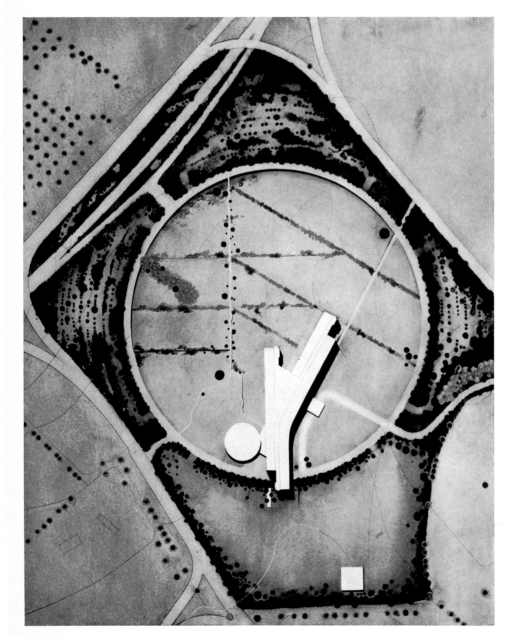

Verwaltungsgebäude der Welt-Gesundheits-organisation, Genf, Entwurf 1960

Der zwölfgeschossige geschwungene Baukörper enthält die Verwaltung, der runde Flachbau den Sitzungssaal. Die von Bäumen beschatteten Parkplätze sind außerhalb der kreisförmigen Grünfläche angelegt. Das Projekt entstand in einem engeren Wettbewerb.

Headquarters Building of the World Health Organisation, Geneva, Project, 1960

The 12-storey curved block contains the offices and the circular low building the conference hall. The tree-shaded car parks are outside the circular open spaces. The project was designed in response to a limited competition.

1 Blick auf die Eingangsfassade.
  View of the entrance side.
2 Lageplan.
  Layout plan.

Nationalbank und Notendruckerei, Kopenhagen, Entwurf 1961

Jacobsens Entwurf erhielt den ersten Preis bei einem begrenzten Wettbewerb. Der Bauplatz liegt im alten Stadtzentrum von Kopenhagen, in der Nähe des Hafens.

National Bank and Bill Printing Plant, Copenhagen, Project, 1961

Jacobsen's design was awarded the First Prize in a limited design competition. The site is situated in Copenhagen's old town centre in the vicinity of the harbour.

1 Lageplan M 1:2000.
  Layout plan, scale 1:2000.
2 Ansicht von Norden.
  View from the North.
3 Ansicht von Südosten.
  View from South-East.

Schokoladenfabrik Tom, Ballerup, 1961

Die Fabrik Tom, die Süßwaren und Schokolade produziert, beschäftigt etwa 500 Arbeiter und 140 Angestellte. Die Neubauten wurden in Ballerup nördlich von Kopenhagen errichtet. Die Anlage, die von Grünflächen und Anpflanzungen umgeben ist, setzt sich zusammen aus dem dreigeschossigen Verwaltungsgebäude am Frederikssundsvej, der großen Fabrikationshalle und der Heizzentrale mit Schmiedewerkstatt. Die flachen Bauten werden überragt von dem Schornstein, von zwei Ölbehältern und den großen Silos für Kakaobohnen. Die Fabrikationshalle erhält durch pyramidenförmige Oberlichter aus Kunstglas Tageslicht.

Tom Chocolate Factory, Ballerup, 1961

The Tom Factory, producing sweets and chocolates, employs some 500 workers and 140 clerical staff. The new buildings were erected at Ballerup, a northern suburb of Copenhagen. The group of buildings, surrounded by open spaces and plantations, consists of the three-storey administration building facing Frederikssundsvej, the large factory hall, and the boiler house with smithy. The low buildings are overtowered by the chimney, two oil tanks, and the large cocoa beans silos. The factory hall receives daylight through pyramid-shaped fanlights of artificial glass.

1 Zylindrische Stahlbetonsilos, im Hintergrund die Ölbehälter aus Stahl.
 Cylindrical reinforced concrete silos and,
 in the background, the oil tanks of steel.
2 Modellansicht.
 Model.

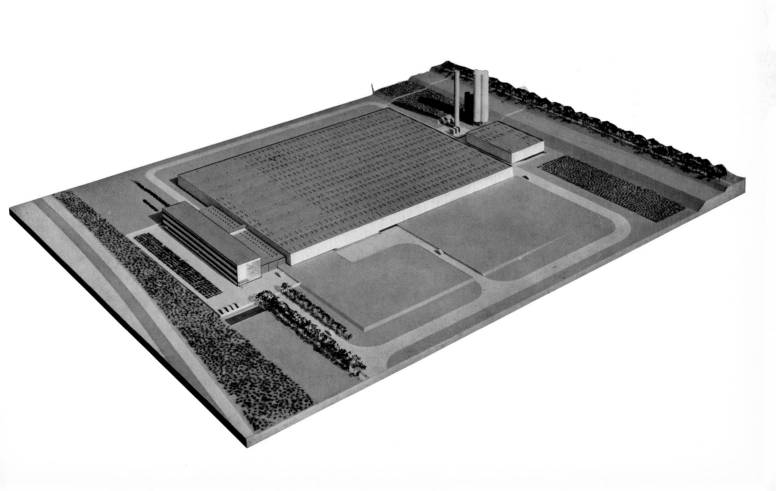

3 Blick auf die mit Dachpappe gedeckte Fabrikationshalle mit den pyramidenförmigen Oberlichtern.
View of the factory hall which is roofed with roofing felt and receives daylight through fanlights.

4 Blick über die Fabrikationshalle auf Schornstein, Silos und Ölbehälter.
View of factory hall with chimney, silos and oil tanks.

5 Ansicht von Süden. Die Außenwände bestehen aus Betonfertigelementen mit ein-
gegossenen weißen Fliesen an der Außenseite.
View from the South. The outer walls consist of pre-fabricated concrete units with
an external facing of white tiles.

6 Ansicht des Verwaltungsgebäudes von
Südosten. Die durchlaufenden Fenster-
bänder werden zur Hälfte durch verstell-
bare Aluminium-Jalousien verdeckt.
View of administration building from South-
East. The continuous window ribbons are
half covered by adjustable aluminium
shutters.

7 Ansicht von Südwesten.
View from South-West.

8, 9 Ansicht des Verwaltungsgebäudes von Osten mit Eingang und Stahltreppe im verglasten Treppenhaus.
View of administration building from the East, with entrance and steel stairs in the glass-enclosed staircase.

Parlamentsgebäude in Islamabad, Pakistan, 1962

Bei diesem Entwurf für das Regierungsviertel der neuen Hauptstadt von Pakistan suchte Jacobsen eine unverwechselbare und von allen Seiten gleich eindrucksvolle Form zu schaffen, die auch die Funktion des Bauwerks zum Ausdruck bringen sollte: über einem niedrigen, langgestreckten, rechtwinkligen Hauptbau erhebt sich ein geschlossener Zylinder, in dem der Parlamentssaal untergebracht ist. Die dreigeschossigen Bürotrakte gruppieren sich um zwei große Innenhöfe, von denen der nordöstliche offen bleiben und im Erdgeschoß als Fußgängerpassage dienen wird, während der südwestliche Hof, in dessen Mitte der zylinderförmige Bau steht, überdacht werden soll. Mitarbeiter: Kaj Blegvad und Peter Denney.

Parliament Building at Islamabad, Pakistan, 1962

With this project for the government precinct of Pakistan's new capital city, Jacobsen's aim was to create an unmistakable design, equally impressive from all sides, which should at the same time express the function of the building: A low, oblong, rectangular block is over-towered by an enclosed cylinder which houses the Parliament Chamber. The three-storey high office buildings are grouped around two large patios; the north-east patio remains open and serves, at ground floor level, as a pedestrian passage whilst the south-west patio, containing the cylindrical building, is to be roofed. Jacobsen was assisted in this project by Kaj Blegvad and Peter Denney.

1 Modellansicht von Südosten. Die Konstruktion besteht durchweg aus Stahlbeton. Die Wände des Bürotraktes werden im Erdgeschoß mit dunklem Marmor verkleidet. Die Fensterzone der beiden Obergeschosse schirmt ein Curtain-Wall aus frei vor die Fassade gehängten Aluminiumplatten ab.
Model, seen from South-East. The structure is of reinforced concrete throughout. The walls of the office block are, at ground floor level, faced with dark marble. The window zone of the two upper floors is screened by a curtain wall which consists of aluminium sheets freely suspended in front of the façade.
2 Modellansicht von Südwesten.
Model, seen from South-West.

144

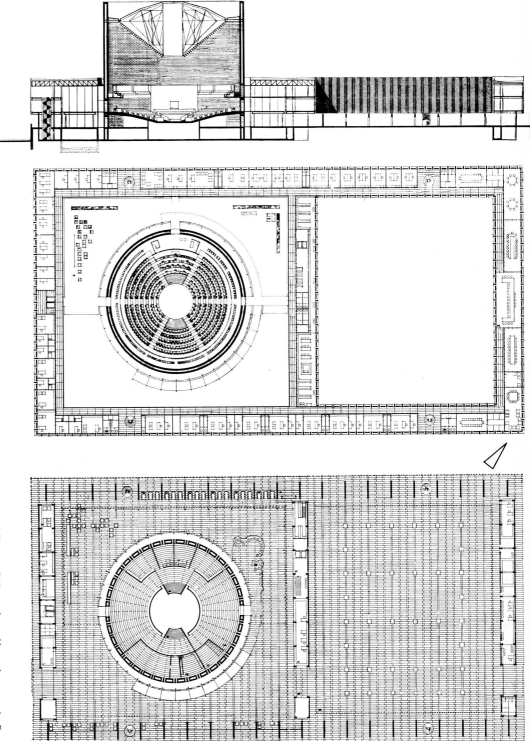

3 Längsschnitt durch Bürotrakte, Parlamentssaal und offenen Nordosthof M 1:1000.
Longitudinal section of office wings, Parliament Chamber and the open north-east patio, scale 1:1000.

4 Grundriß von Bürogeschoß und Parlamentssaal M 1:1000.
Plan of office floor and Parliament Chamber, scale 1:1000.

5 Grundriß von Erdgeschoß und Moschee unter dem Parlamentssaal M 1:1000.
Plan of ground floor and mosque below the Parliament Chamber, scale 1:1000.

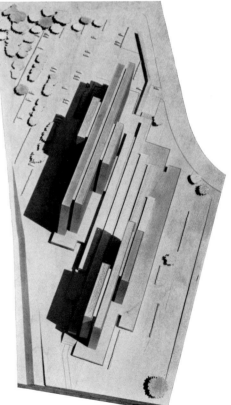

Verwaltungsgebäude der Hamburgischen Electricitätswerke, 1962

Bei dem 1962 ausgeschriebenen Wettbewerb für ein Vorprojekt kam Jacobsens Entwurf mit drei anderen Arbeiten in die engere Wahl. Einen zweiten Wettbewerb unter diesen vier Architekten konnte er mit der hier wiedergegebenen Lösung gewinnen, die sich übrigens vom ersten Projekt nicht prinzipiell unterscheidet. Der Entwurf sieht über einem niedrigen Sockel, der den Großteil des Grundstücks einnimmt, zwei scheibenförmige Hochhausgruppen vor, von denen zunächst nur die östliche ausgeführt werden soll. Im niedrigen Bauteil sind die Räume mit Publikumsverkehr zusammengefaßt, während die interne Verwaltung in den Hochbauten untergebracht wird. Der Keller soll als Tiefgarage ausgebaut werden, weitere Parkflächen bietet das Erdgeschoß, so daß insgesamt 700 Wagen abgestellt werden können. Im Erdgeschoß sind ferner ein Vortragssaal, Registratur- und Personalräume sowie die Kantine untergebracht. Im ersten Obergeschoß umzieht eine Fußgänger-Plattform die Hochbauten. Die Ausführung ist in Stahlbeton vorgesehen. Bei den Hochhausscheiben besteht die Tragkonstruktion aus Stützen zu beiden Seiten des Mittelgangs, die auskragenden Geschoßdecken sollen aus vorfabrizierten Betonelementen montiert werden. Die Fassadenelemente setzen sich aus eloxierten Aluminiumprofilen mit doppelwandigen Glasfüllungen zusammen, zwischen denen automatisch gesteuerte Sonnenschutzlamellen angebracht sind. Mitarbeiter bei diesem Projekt waren Otto Weitling und Lasse Halskov; Folmer Andersen wirkte als beratender Ingenieur.

Headquarters Building of the Hamburg Electricity Supply Company, 1962

As a result of a preliminary design competition held in 1962, Jacobsen's design together with three others came on the short list. A second competition among these four architects was won by him with the project here reproduced which incidentally does not differ, in principle, from his first project. It envisages a low building, covering most of the site, overtowered by two pier-shaped clusters of multi-storey blocks, of which only the one in the east is to be built at present. The low building contains all the premises open to the public whilst the internal administration is housed in the tower blocks. The basement is to serve as an underground garage, and further parking facilities are to be provided at ground floor level so that, altogether, 700 cars can be parked. The ground floor also contains a lecture room, a records section, staff premises, and canteen. At first floor level, the tower blocks are surrounded by pedestrian walkways. The buildings are to be erected in reinforced concrete. In the case of the tower blocks, the bearing structure consists of columns on either side of the central corridor, carrying cantilevered floor slabs assembled from prefabricated concrete units. The façade units consist of anodically treated aluminium profiles with double panes of glass; mounted between these panes are automatically controlled Venetian blinds. Consulting Engineer: Folmer Andersen. Assistants: Otto Weitling and Lasse Halskov.

1 Modellansicht von Osten.
  Model, seen from the East.
2 Aufsicht auf das Modell von Norden.
  Bird's eye view of the model from the North.

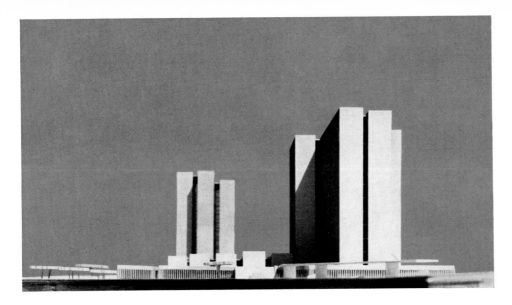

3 Modellansicht von Süden.
   Model, seen from the South.
4 Grundriß Erdgeschoß M 1:1500.
   Ground floor plan, scale 1:1500.
5 Grundriß erstes Obergeschoß M 1:1500.
   First floor plan, scale 1:1500.
6 Querschnitt A-A M 1:1500.
   Cross section A-A, scale 1:1500.
7 Östliches Bürohochhaus, Grundriß Normalgeschoß M 1:1500.
   Typical floor plan of the East Tower, scale 1:1500.

1 Parkfläche / Parking area
2 Lager-, Registratur- und Büchereiräume
   Stores, records and accounts
3 Speisesaal / Dining room
4 Vortragssaal / Lecture room
5 Ausstellungsräume / Showrooms
6 Eingang / Entrance
7 Büroräume mit Kundenverkehr
   Offices open to the public
8 Vorraum Aufzüge / Lift landing
9 Bürosaal / Offices

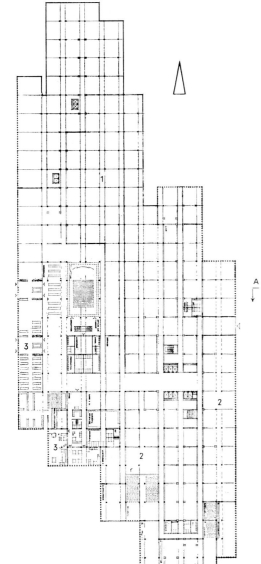

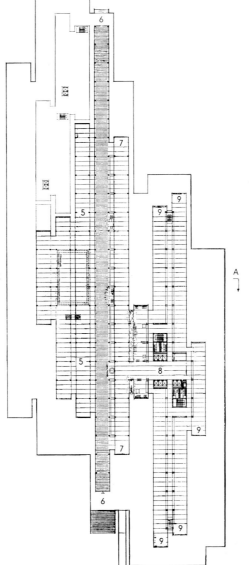

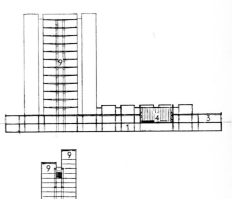

1 Besteck aus rostfreiem Stahl. 1957. Entworfen für den Hofjuwelier A. Michelsen.
Stainless steel cutlery, 1957, designed for Crown Jeweller A. Michelsen.

2 Aschenbecher und Kerzenhalter. Entworfen für das SAS-Hotel.
Ashtray and candlestick, designed for the SAS hotel.

3 Versilberte Salz- und Pfefferstreuer und Senftöpfchen. Entworfen für das SAS-Hotel.
Silver-plated condiment set, designed for the SAS hotel.

4 Versilbertes Eßbesteck. Entworfen für das SAS-Hotel. Das Besteck wird in der Snackbar verwendet.
Silver-plated cutlery, designed for the SAS hotel. The cutlery is used in the snack bar.

5 Aschenbecher aus Porzellan. 1960. Entwor-
fen für das SAS-Hotel.
China ashtrays, 1960, designed for the
SAS hotel.

6 Zeichnung für Tischgläser. Die Gläser, die für Restaurant und Bar des SAS-Hotels bestimmt sind, wurden so entworfen, daß sie in der Spülmaschine besonders leicht gereinigt werden können.
Design for table glassware. The glasses, destined for the restaurant and bar of the SAS hotel, were specially designed for ease of cleaning in the dishwasher.

1 Ausstellungsstand für Lavenda Strickwolle auf der britischen Ausstellung in Kopenhagen, 1955.
Exhibition stand for Lavenda Knitting Wool at the British Exhibition in Copenhagen, 1955.
2 Ausstellungsvitrine auf der Ausstellung H 55 in Helsingborg, 1955.
Display unit for the H 55 Exhibition at Helsingborg, 1955.

1, 2 Hängelampe aus rauchfarbenem Plexiglas. Entworfen für die Bar des SAS-
Hotels.
Pendant lamp of smoke-coloured Plexiglass, designed for the bar of the SAS
hotel.

3 Stehlampe aus braun lackiertem Metall.
Schirm aus leinenbeklebtem Kunststoff.
Entworfen für das SAS-Hotel.
Standard lamp of brown-varnished metal
and cloth-lined plastics, designed for the
SAS hotel.

15

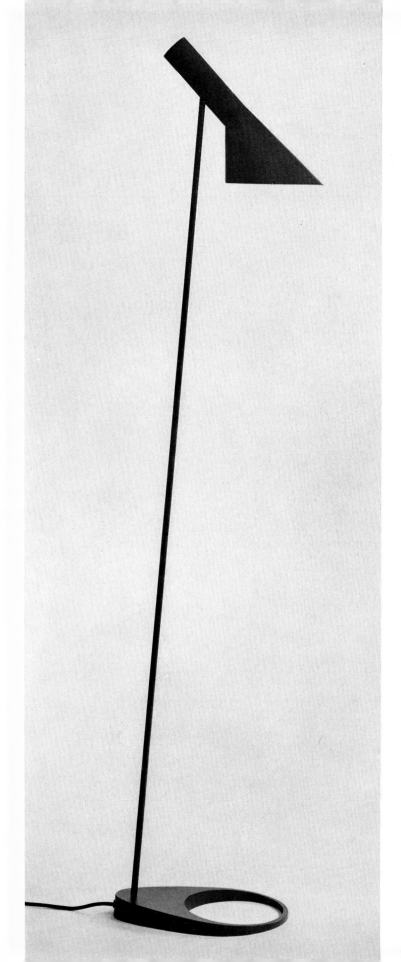

4 Stehlampe aus schwarz lackiertem Metall. 1957. Unter anderem im SAS-Hotel verwendet.
Standard lamp of black-varnished metal, 1957, used (inter alia) in the SAS hotel.

5 Deckenlampe aus weißem Opalglas mit Messingrand. 1955. Entworfen für die Munkegårds-Schule.
Ceiling lamp of white opal glass with brass fitting, 1955, designed for Munkegårds School.

6 Wandlampe aus weißem Opalglas.
Wall mounted lamp of white opal glass.

7 Pendelleuchte. Der Metallschirm ist in verschiedenen Farben erhältlich.
Pendant lamp; the metal shade is available in different colours.
Alle diese Lampen wurden für die Firma Louis Poulsen & Co. entworfen.
All these lamps were designed for Messrs. Louis Poulsen & Co.

8 Lautsprecher. Entworfen für die Firma Poul Lehmbeck. Silbermedaille der Mailänder Triennale 1957.
Loudspeaker, designed for Messrs. Poul Lehmbeck. Awarded a Silver Medal at the Milan Triennale, 1957.

15

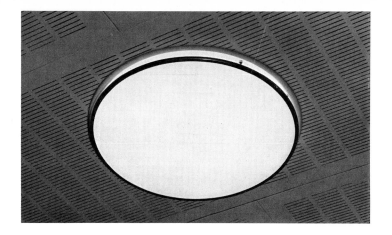

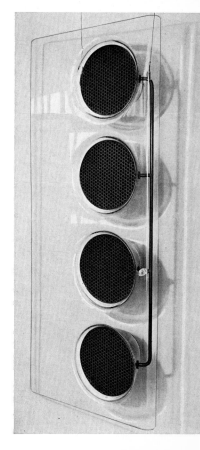

1 Stoffdruckmuster »Ampfer«. 1942-43.
"Dockleaves" design for textile prints,
1942-43.

2 Stoffdruck- und Tapetenmuster »Schilf«.
1942-43.
"Reed" design for textile prints and wall
paper, 1942-43.

3 Stoffdruckmuster »Fuchsschwänze«.
1942-43.
"Fox tails" design for textile prints,
1942-43.

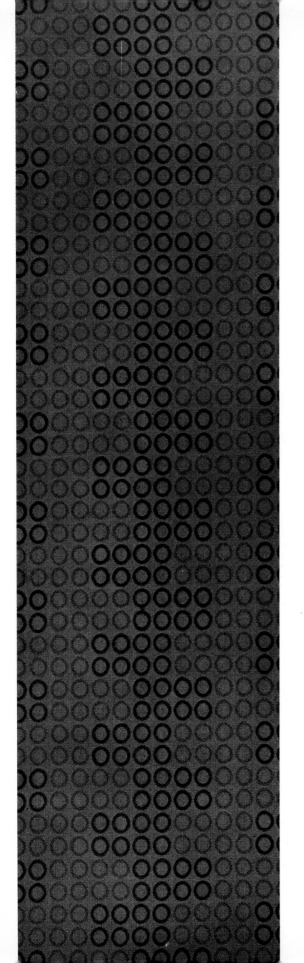

4 Bodenteppich. Entworfen für das SAS-
Hotel.
  Carpet, designed for the SAS hotel.
5 Stoffdruckmuster »Tasco«.
  "Tasco" design for textile prints.
6 Stoffdruckmuster »Wellenlinie«.
  "Wave line" design for textile prints.

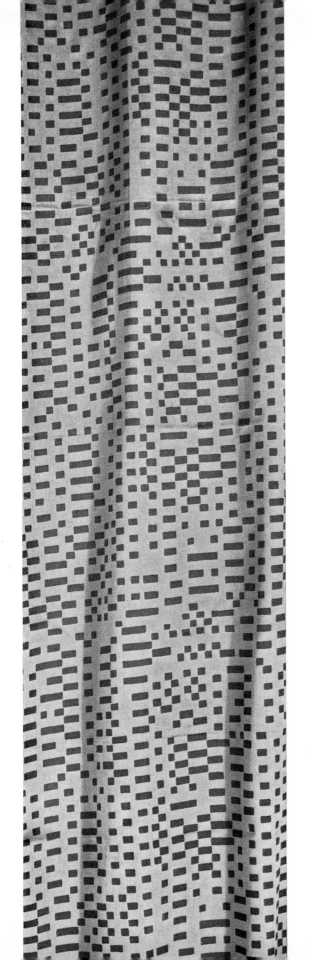

Möbel / Furniture

1 Sitzreihen des Bellevue-Theaters aus
verformtem Schichtholz. 1935.
Rows of seats for the Bellevue Theatre,
made of shaped laminated wood, 1935.
2 Dreibeiniger Stapelstuhl. 1952. Entworfen
für die Firma Fritz Hansens Nachf.
Three-legged stacking chair, 1952;
designed for Messrs. Fritz Hansens Eftf.

3, 4 Sessel »Kuhle«. Gestell aus Stahlrohr,
Sitz und Rücken mit Leder bezogen. Entworfen für das SAS-Gebäude.
"Bow" armchair; tubular steel frame,
leather-covered seat and back. Designed
for the SAS building.

5 Tisch und Stühle aus verformtem Schichtholz mit hoher Rückenlehne. Entworfen für
den Speisesaal des St. Catherine's College, Oxford. 1963.
Table and chairs with high backs, made of
shaped laminated wood, designed for the
Refectory of St. Catherine's College,
Oxford, 1963.

6 Lehnstuhl und Hocker aus verformtem
Schichtholz, mit Eiche furniert. Entworfen
für die Schülerzimmer des St. Catherine's
College.
Armchair and stool of shaped laminated
wood, veneered with oak. Designed for
the undergraduates' rooms at St. Catherine's College.

7 Ruhesessel »Das Ei«. Die Schale aus
  leichtem Kunststoff ist mit Stoff bezogen,
  der Drehfuß aus Stahl. 1959. Entworfen
  für die Firma Fritz Hansens Nachf.
  "The Egg" chair. The shell is made of
  light, cloth-covered plastics, and the base
  of the revolving chair of steel, 1959, designed for Messrs. Fritz Hansens Eftf.
8 Ruhesessel »Schwan«. Kunststoffschale
  mit Lederbezug. 1959. Entworfen für die
  Firma Fritz Hansens Nachf.
  "Swan" armchair. Plastics shell with
  leather cover, 1959, designed for
  Messrs. Fritz Hansens Eftf.

9, 10 Stuhl und Schreibtisch. Entworfen für die American-Scandinavian Foundation, New York. Stiftung der Werft Burmeister & Wain. Hersteller des Schreibtisches ist die Schreinerei Rudolf Rasmussen. Chair and desk, designed for the American-Scandinavian Foundation, New York; a donation by the shipbuilders, Burmeister & Wain. (Manufacturer of the desk: Rudolf Rasmussen, Cabinetmakers.)

11 Stuhl aus verformtem Schichtholz. Entworfen für die Firma Fritz Hansens Nachf. Großer Preis auf der Mailänder Triennale 1957.
Chair made of shaped laminated wood, designed for Messrs. Fritz Hansens Eftf. Grand Prix at the Milan Triennale, 1957.

12-14 Vierbeiniger Stapelstuhl. 1955. Entworfen für die Firma Fritz Hansens Nachf.
Four-legged stacking chair, 1955, designed for Messrs. Fritz Hansens Eftf.

Gärten / Gardens

Gartenhöfe mit wechselnder Bepflanzung und verschiedenen Plattenbelägen in der Munkegårds-Schule, Gentofte (Seite 60). 1952-56.
Patios with variegated plantation and different flag pavings at Munkegårds School, Gentofte (page 60), 1952-56.

1 Verschiedene Binsenarten, zwischen den Bodenplatten Cotula (Fiederpolster).
Different species of rushes and, between the flags, Cotula.
2 Pyrakantos (Feuerdorn) und Sagina (Sternmoos).
Pyracanth and Sagina.
3 Nadelbaum, der im Winter die Nadeln verliert, und Sagina (Sternmoos) zwischen den Bodenplatten.
Defoliating conifer and, between the flags, Sagina.
4 Zwischen den Bodenplatten Cotula (Fiederpolster).
Between the flags: Cotula.
5 Cotorne-Astern mit Sagina (Sternmoos).
Cotorneaster with Sagina.

1

2

3

4

5

6 Garten für Edwin Jensen im Mosehøjvej,
  Ordrup (Seite 22). 1960.
  Garden for Edwin Jensen at Mosehøjvej,
  Ordrup (page 22), 1960.

7, 8 Garten für Harald Pedersen in der
     Dronningsgårds Allé. 1935.
     Garden for Harald Pedersen at Dron-
     ningsgårds Allé, 1935.
9 Garten für Thorvald Pedersen im Konge-
  højen, Klampenborg. 1938.
  Garden for Thorvald Pedersen at Konge-
  højen, Klampenborg, 1938.

10-12 Arne Jacobsens eigener Garten in der
Siedlung Søholm, Klampenborg, 1950.
Arne Jacobsen's own garden at the Sø-
holm Housing Estate, Klampenborg, 1950.   17

13, 14 Garten für Ruthwen Jürgensen, Vedbæk. 1956.
Garden for Ruthwen Jürgensen. Vedbæk, 1956.

Fotonachweis

Aero Express, Kopenhagen: 29. Bent Andersen, Kopenhagen: 152, Th. Andresen, Kopenhagen: XIII (rechts). Hammerschmidt-Foto, Århus: 86, 87. Erik Hansen, Kopenhagen: 163, 168 (oben). Jesper Høm, Kopenhagen: 156. Jonals Co., Kopenhagen: VIII (rechts), 30, 34. K. Hellmer-Petersen, Kopenhagen: 157 (oben rechts), 166 (unten). Maarbjergs Atelier, Gentofte: 81. Rigmor Mydtskov, Kopenhagen: 108, 144. Rading, Kopenhagen: XI (links), X (rechts), 35 (oben). Stadtbildstelle, Essen: 109. Strüwing Reklamefoto, Kopenhagen: XIII (links), 3-7, 11 (oben), 12, 14, 15, 17 (oben), 19-27, 31, 37, 39-57, 60, 62-67, 70-79, 83-85, 88-107, 110-143, 148-150, 154, 155, 157 (oben links und unten rechts), 158-161, 164, 165 (unten), 166 (oben), 167, 168 (unten links), 169, 170, 171 (oben), 172 (unten), 173, Umschlag.